PENGUIN BOOKS

THREE THOUSAND STITCHES

Sudha Murty was born in 1950 in Shiggaon, north Karnataka. She did her MTech in computer science, and is now the chairperson of the Infosys Foundation. A prolific writer in English and Kannada, she has written novels, technical books, travelogues, collections of short stories and non-fictional pieces, and four books for children. Her books have been translated into all the major Indian languages. Sudha Murty was the recipient of the R.K. Narayan Award for Literature and the Padma Shri in 2006, and the Attimabbe Award from the government of Karnataka for excellence in Kannada literature, in 2011.

BY THE SAME AUTHOR

FICTION

Dollar Bahu
Mahashweta
Gently Falls the Bakula
House of Cards
The Mother I Never Knew

NON-FICTION

Wise and Otherwise
The Old Man and His God
The Day I Stopped Drinking Milk
*Something Happened on the Way to Heaven: Twenty
Inspiring Real-Life Stories* (Ed.)

CHILDREN'S FICTION

How I Taught My Grandmother to Read and Other Stories
The Magic Drum and Other Favourite Stories
The Bird with Golden Wings: Stories of Wit and Magic
Grandma's Bag of Stories
The Serpent's Revenge: Unusual Tales from the Mahabharata
The Magic of the Lost Temple

SUDHA MURTY

THREE THOUSAND STITCHES

Ordinary People, Extraordinary Lives

PENGUIN BOOKS

PENGUIN BOOKS

USA | Canada | UK | Ireland | Australia
New Zealand | India | South Africa | China

Penguin Books is part of the Penguin Random House group of companies
whose addresses can be found at global.penguinrandomhouse.com

Published by Penguin Random House India Pvt. Ltd
7th Floor, Infinity Tower C, DLF Cyber City,
Gurgaon 122 002, Haryana, India

Penguin
Random House
India

First published in Penguin Books by Penguin Random House India 2017

Copyright © Sudha Murty 2017

10 9 8 7 6 5 4 3 2 1

The views and opinions expressed in this book are the author's own and the
facts are as reported by her which have been verified to the extent possible,
and the publishers are not in any way liable for the same.

ISBN 9780143440055

Typeset in Dante MT Std by Manipal Digital Systems, Manipal
Printed at Thomson Press India Ltd, New Delhi

www.penguin.co.in

Contents

Preface   ix

1. Three Thousand Stitches   1
2. How to Beat the Boys   17
3. Food for Thought   33
4. Three Handfuls of Water   47
5. Cattle Class   65
6. A Life Unwritten   73
7. No Place Like Home   85
8. A Powerful Ambassador   105
9. Rasleela and the Swimming Pool   119
10. A Day in Infosys Foundation   133
11. I Can't, We Can   153

Preface

I often get letters from students and parents telling me how beneficial my books have been for them and their children. I want to thank them and all those who have exposed me to different facets of life, filling my pot of learning with knowledge and experience. This includes the young men and women who have shown me how they put aside their bitter experiences to move forward in life with joy and hope.

There are some who feel that most of my writing is fiction, but my life has unmistakably proven to be stranger than that.

Fifteen years ago, renowned journalist T.J.S. George asked me to write a weekly column for the *New Indian Express*. I was hesitant at first—all because I was educated in a Kannada-medium school till the tenth grade. It was only natural then that I was more comfortable with Kannada than English. George said to me, 'A language is but a vehicle. It's the person inside who's weaving the story that's more important. You are a storyteller. So just get on with your story and the language will fall into place.'

And so began my journey in English. I am what I am today as an English author because of George. He gave me the title of my first book, *Wise and Otherwise,* and wrote the foreword too. His foresight and encouragement catapulted me from a hesitant writer to a widely read author.

I often dream about the world being filled with many Georges who will come forward to support such writers and encourage them to experiment and explore their potential.

I want to thank my young and bright editor, Shrutkeerti Khurana, and also Udayan Mitra and Meru Gokhale for bringing out this book.

1

Three Thousand Stitches

We set up the Infosys Foundation in 1996. Unfortunately, I knew precious little of how things worked in a non-profit organization. I knew more about software, management, programming and tackling software bugs. Examinations, mark sheets and deadlines occupied most of my days. The concept behind the foundation was that it must make a difference to the common man—*bahujan hitaya, bahujan sukhaya*—it must provide compassionate aid regardless of caste, creed, language or religion.

As we pondered over the issues before us—malnutrition, education, rural development, self-sufficiency, access to medicine, cultural activities and the revival of the arts, among others—there was one issue that occupied my uppermost thoughts—the devadasi tradition that was pervasive throughout India.

The word devadasi means 'servant of the Lord'. Traditionally, devadasis were musicians and dancers who practised their craft in temples to please the gods. They had a high status in society. We can see the evidence of it in the caves of Badami, as well as in stories like that of the devadasi Vinapodi, who was very dear to the ruling king of the Chalukya dynasty between the sixth and seventh century in northern Karnataka. The king donated enormous sums of money to temples. However, as time went by, the temples were destroyed and the tradition of the devadasis fell into the wrong hands. Young girls were initially dedicated to the worship and service of a deity or a temple in good faith, but eventually, the word devadasi became synonymous with sex worker. Some were born into the life, while others were 'sacrificed' to the temples by their parents due to various reasons, or simply because they caught a hair infection like the ringworm of the scalp, assumed to be indicative that the girl was destined to be a devadasi.

As I thought about their plight, I recalled my visit to the Yellamma Gudda (or Renuka temple) in the Belgaum district of Karnataka years ago. I remembered their green saris and bangles, the smears of yellow *bhandara* (a coarse turmeric powder) and their thick, long hair as they entered the temple with goddess masks, coconuts, neem leaves and a *kalash* (a metal pot). 'Why can't I tackle this problem?' I wondered. I didn't realize then that I was choosing one of the most difficult tasks for our very first project.

With innocence and bubbling enthusiasm, I chose a place in northern Karnataka where the practice was rampant and prostitution was carried on in the name of religion. My plan was to talk to the devadasis and write down their concerns to help me understand their predicament, followed by organizing a few discussions targeted towards solving their problems within a few months.

On my first day in the district, I armed myself with a notebook and pen and set out. I dressed simply, with no jewellery or bindi. I wore a pair of jeans, T-shirt and a cap. After some time, I found a group of devadasis sitting below a tree near a temple. They were chatting and removing lice from each other's hair.

Without thinking, I went up to them, interrupting their conversation. '*Namaskaram*, Amma. I've come here to help you. Tell me your problems and I'll write them down.'

They must have been discussing something important because the women gave me a dirty look. They lobbed questions at me with increasing ferocity.

'Who are you? Did we invite you here?'

'Have you come to write about us? In that case, we don't want to talk to you.'

'Are you an officer? Or a minister? If we tell you our problems, how will you solve them?'

'Go away. Go back to where you came from.'

I did not move. In fact, I persisted. 'I want to help you. Please listen to me. Are you aware that there is a dangerous illness called AIDS that you could be exposed to? There is no cure for . . .'

'Just go,' one of them snapped. I glanced at their faces. They were furious.

But I did not leave. 'Maybe they need a little convincing,' I thought.

Without warning, one of them stood up, took off her chappal and threw it at me. 'Can't you understand simple Kannada? Just get lost.'

Insulted and humiliated, I felt my tears threatening to spill over. I turned back and fled.

Upon returning home, with the insult fresh on my mind, I told myself, 'I won't go there again.'

However, a few days later, it occurred to me that the women were probably upset about something else and that maybe I had simply chosen the wrong time and date to visit them.

So after another week, I went there again. This visit took place during the tomato harvest. The devadasi women were happily distributing small, oval-shaped bright red tomatoes to each other from the baskets kept near them. I approached them and smiled pleasantly. 'Hello, I've come to meet you again! Please hear me out. I really, really want to help you.'

They laughed at me. 'We don't need your help. But would you like to buy some tomatoes?'

'No, I am not very fond of tomatoes.'

'What kind of a woman are you? Who doesn't like tomatoes?'

I attempted to engage them once more, 'Have you heard of AIDS? You must know that the government is spending a lot of money on increasing awareness about it.'

'Are you a government agent? Or maybe you belong to a political party. How much commission are you getting to do this? Come on, tell us! We don't even have a proper hospital in this area and here you are, trying to educate us about a scary disease. We don't need your help. Our goddess will help us in difficult times.'

I stood dumbfounded, struggling to find words.

One of the women said decisively, 'This lady must be a journalist. That's why she has a pen and paper. She'll write about us and make money by exploiting us.' Upon hearing this, the others started throwing tomatoes at me.

This time, my emotions overpowered me and I started to cry. Sobbing, I fled from there once again.

I was in despair. 'Why should I work on this project? Why do they keep insulting me? Where else do the beneficiaries humiliate the person working for their well-being? I am not a good fit for this field. Yes, I should resign and go back to my academic career. The foundation can choose a different trustee.'

When I reached home, I sat down to compose a resignation letter.

My father came down the stairs and seeing me busy with my head bent close to the paper, he asked, 'What are you writing so frantically?'

I narrated the entire episode to him.

To my amazement, rather than sympathizing with me, my father chuckled and said, 'I didn't know that you were so impractical.'

I stared at him in anger.

He took an ice cream from the fridge and forced me to sit down and eat it. 'It'll cool your head,' he said and smiled. After a few minutes, he said, 'Please remember. Prostitution has existed in society since ancient times and has become an integral part of life. It is one of the root problems of all civilizations. Many kings and saints have tried to eliminate it but no law or punishment has been successful in bringing it down to zero. Not one nation in the world is free of this. Then how can you change the entire system by yourself? You're just an ordinary woman! What you should do is reduce your expectations and lower your goal. For instance, try to help ten devadasis leave their profession. Rehabilitate them and show them what it means to lead a normal life. This will guarantee that their children will not follow in their footsteps. Make that your aim, and the day you accomplish it, I will feel very proud knowing that I gave birth to a daughter who helped ten helpless women make the most difficult transition from being sex workers to independent women.'

'But they threw chappals and tomatoes at me, Kaka,' I whined petulantly. I always called my father 'Kaka'.

'Actually, you got a promotion today—from chappals to tomatoes. If you pursue this and go there a third time, maybe you'll get something even better!' His joke brought a reluctant smile to my face.

'They won't even talk to me. Then how can I work for them?'

'Look at yourself,' my father said, dragging me in front of the nearest mirror. 'You are casually dressed in a T-shirt, a pair of jeans and a cap. This may be your style, but the common man and a rural Indian woman like the devadasi will never connect or identify with you. If you wear a sari, a *mangalsutra*, put on a bindi and tie your hair, I'm sure that they will receive you much better than before. I'll also come with you. An old man like me will be of great help to you in such an adventure.'

I protested, 'I don't want to alter my appearance for their sake. I don't believe in such superficial changes.'

'Well, if you want to change them, then you have to change yourself first. Change your attitude. Of course, it's your decision in the end.'

He left me in front of the mirror and walked away.

My parents had never thrust their choices or beliefs on me or any of my siblings, whether it was about education, profession or marriage. They always gave their advice and helped us if we wanted, but I made all the choices.

For a few days, I was confused. I thought about the skills needed for social work. There was no glamour or money in this profession and I could not behave like an executive in a corporate house. I required language skills, of which English may not be needed at all! I should be able to sit down on the floor and eat the local food, no matter where I travelled for work. I had to listen patiently, and most of all, I should love the work I did. What would give me higher satisfaction—keeping my external appearance the way it was or the work that I would do?

After some introspection, I decided to change my appearance and concentrate completely on the work.

Before my next visit, I pulled my hair back, tied it and adorned it with flowers. I wore a two-hundred-rupee sari, a big bindi, a mangalsutra and glass bangles. I transformed myself into the 'bharatiya nari', the stereotypical traditional Indian woman, and took my father along with me to meet the devadasis.

This time, when we went there, upon seeing my aged father, they said, 'Namaste.'

My father introduced me. 'This is my daughter and she is a teacher. She has come here on a holiday. I told her how difficult your lives are. Your children are the reason for your existence and you want to educate them irrespective of what happens to your health, am I right?'

They replied in unison, 'Yes, sir!'

'Since my daughter is a teacher, she can guide you with your children's education and help them find better jobs. She'll give you information about some scholarships which you may not be aware of and help your kids with it so that your financial burden may be reduced. Is that okay with you? If not, it's all right. She'll go to some other village and try to help the people there. Please don't feel pressured. Think about it and get back to us. We'll be back in ten minutes.'

Grasping my hand tightly, he pulled me a short distance away.

'Why did you say all that?' I asked. 'You should have first told them about things like the dangers of AIDS.'

'Don't be foolish. We will tell them about it some other time. If you start with something negative, then nobody will like it. The first introduction should always be positive and bring real hope to the beneficiary. And just like I've promised them, you must help their children get scholarships first. Work on AIDS later.'

'And why did you tell them I'm a teacher, Kaka?' I demanded. 'You could have said I was a social worker.'

My father offered a calm rebuttal. 'They consider teaching to be one of the most respectable jobs and you are a professor, aren't you?'

I nodded reluctantly, still unsure of his strategy.

When we went back, the women were ready to listen. They called me *akka* or 'elder sister' in Kannada.

So I started working with them to help their children secure the promised scholarships. Some of these children even started going to college within a year. Only after this happened did I bring up the subject of AIDS, and this time, they heard me out. Months went by. It took me almost three years to establish a relationship with them. I was their darling akka and eventually, they trusted me enough to share their heart-touching stories and the trials they had endured.

Innocent girls had been sold into the trade by their husbands, brothers, fathers, boyfriends, uncles or other relatives. Some entered the sex trade on their own hoping to earn some money for their families and help future generations escape poverty. Still others were lured into it with the promise of a real job, only to find themselves tricked to work as sex workers. Hearing their stories, there were moments when I couldn't hide my tears, yet they were the ones who held my hand and consoled me! Each story was different but the end was the same—they all suffered at the hands of a society that exploited them and filled them with guilt and shame as a final insult.

I realized that simply donating money would not bolster their confidence or build their self-esteem. The best solution

I could think of was to unite them towards a common goal by helping them build their own organization. The state government of Karnataka had many good policies that encouraged housing, marriage schemes and scholarships, but if we started an association or a union exclusively for the devadasis, they could address each other's problems. In time, they would become bold and independent, learning to organize themselves in the process.

Thus, an organization for the devadasis was formed. I believe that God cannot be present everywhere at once and, in return, he sends people to do his work. Abhay Kumar, a kind-hearted and idealistic young man from Delhi, joined us unexpectedly. He wanted to work with me and so I decided to give him the toughest job in order to test his passion for social work. I told Abhay, 'If you work with the devadasis for eight months and survive, I'll think about absorbing you into the project full-time.'

As promised, he did not show up for eight months, and then one day, he confidently strolled into my office, a little thinner, but grinning from ear to ear.

I said, 'Abhay, now you know how hard social work is. It takes extreme commitment and persistence to keep going. You can go back to Delhi with the satisfaction of having made a difference to so many lives. You are a good human being and I'm sure that this little experience will stay with you and help you later.'

He smiled and replied in impeccable Kannada, 'Who said that I wanted to go back to Delhi? I've decided to stay in Karnataka and complete this project.'

'Abhay, this is serious work. You are young and that's a great disadvantage in this line of work and . . .' My voice faded away. I didn't know what else to say!

'Don't worry about that, ma'am! You gave me the best job I could possibly have. I thought that you might give me a desk job. I never imagined that you'd give me fieldwork, that too, the privilege of working with the devadasis. This past year has made me realize their agony and unbearable hardships. Knowing that, how can I ever work anywhere apart from here?'

I was astonished at such sincerity and compassion in one so young. I offered him a stipend to help with his expenses but he stopped me with a show of his hand, 'I don't need that much. I already have a scooter and a few sets of clothes. I just need two meals a day, a roof over my head and a little money for petrol. That's it.'

I gazed at him fondly and knew that I was seeing a man who had found his purpose in life. He bid goodbye and left my office with determined strides.

Obviously, Abhay became the project lead, and I supported him wholeheartedly, taking care to converse with him regularly about the project's progress.

One day, I met with the devadasis and inquired about the welfare of their children.

'Our greatest difficulty is supporting our children's education,' they said. 'Most of the time, we can't afford their school fees and then we have to go back to what we know to get quick money.'

'We will take care of all your children's educational expenses irrespective of which class they are in. But that means that you must not continue being a devadasi, no matter what,' I replied firmly.

The women agreed without hesitation. They had come to trust Abhay and me and knew that we would keep our word.

Hundreds of children were enrolled in the project—some went on to do professional courses while others went on to complete their primary, middle or high school classes. We held camps on AIDS awareness and prevention and sponsored street art and plays to educate the women and children on various medical issues—including the simple fact that infected hair is not an indication that one must become a devadasi. Rather, it is a simple curable disease that causes the hair to stick together and become matted over time. The women got themselves treated and some of them even had their heads shaved.

Eventually, we were able to get them loans by becoming their guarantors. Often, the women would tell me, 'Akka, please help us get a loan. If we can't repay it, then it is as good as cheating you and you know that we'll never do that.' By this time I knew in my heart that a rich man might cheat me but our devadasis never would. They had great faith in me and I in them.

On the other hand, life became more dangerous for Abhay and me. We received death threats from pimps, local goons and others through phone calls, letters and messages. I was scared more for Abhay than myself. Though I asked for police protection, Abhay flatly refused and said, 'Our devadasis will protect me. Don't worry about me.'

A few weeks later, some pimps threw acid on three devadasis who had left their profession for good. But we all still refused to give up. The plastic surgery the victims underwent helped to bring back their confidence. They would not be intimidated. Our strength came from these women who were collectively trying to leave this hated profession. Though the government supplemented their income, many also started rearing goats, cows and buffaloes.

Over time, we established small schools that offered night classes which the devadasis could attend. It was an uphill battle that took years of effort from everybody involved. After twelve years, some of the women met me to discuss a particular issue.

'Akka, we want to start a bank, but we are afraid to do it on our own.'

'What do you think happens in a bank?' I asked.

'Well, you need a lot of money to start a bank or even have an account. You must wear expensive clothes. We've seen that bankers usually wear suits and ties and sit in air-conditioned offices, but we don't have money for such things, Akka.'

After they brought this problem to our attention, Abhay and I sat down with the women and explained the basics of banking to them. A few professionals were consulted, and under their guidance, they started a bank of their own, with the exception of a few legal and administrative services that we provided. However, we insisted that the bank employees and shareholders should be restricted only to the devadasi community. So finally, the women were able to save money through fixed deposits and obtain low-interest loans. All profits had to be shared with the bank members. Eventually, the bank grew and the women themselves became its directors and took over its running.

Less than three years later, the bank had Rs 80 lakh in deposits and provided employment to former devadasis, but its most important achievement was that almost 3000 women were out of the devadasi system.

On their third anniversary, I received a letter from the bank.

We are very happy to share that three years have passed since the bank was started. Now, the bank is of sound financial health and none of us practise or make any money through the devadasi tradition. We have each paid a hundred rupees and have three lakhs saved for a big celebration. We have rented out a hall and arranged lunch for everyone. Please come and join us for our big day. Akka, you are very dear to us and we want you to be our chief guest for the occasion. You have travelled hundreds of times at your own cost and spent endless money for our sake even though we are strangers. This time, we want to book a round-trip air-conditioned Volvo bus ticket, a good hotel and an all-expenses-paid trip for you. Our money has been earned legally, ethically and morally. We are sure that you won't refuse our humble and earnest request.

Tears welled up in my eyes. Seventeen years ago, chappals were my reward, but now, they wanted to pay for my travel to the best of their ability. I knew how much the comfort of an air-conditioned Volvo bus and a hotel meant to them.

I decided to attend the function at my expense.

On the day of the function, I found that there were no politicians or garlands or long speeches as was typical. It was a simple event. At first, some women sang a song of agony written by the devadasis. Then another group came and described their experiences on their journey to independence. Their children, many of whom had become doctors, nurses, lawyers, clerks, government employees, teachers, railway employees and bank officers, came and thanked their mothers and the organization for supporting their education.

And then it was my turn to speak.

I stood there, and my words suddenly failed me. My mind went blank, and then, distantly, I remembered my father's words: 'I will feel very proud knowing that I gave birth to a daughter who helped ten helpless women make the most difficult transition from being sex workers to independent women.'

I am usually a spontaneous speaker but on that day, I was too choked with emotion. I didn't know where to begin. For the first time in my life, I felt that the day I meet God, I will be able to stand up straight and say confidently, 'You've given me a lot in this lifetime, and I hope that I have returned at least something. I've served 3000 of your children in the best way I could, relieving them of the meaningless and cruel devadasi system. Your children are your flowers and I am returning them to you.'

Then my eyes fell on the women. They were so eager to listen to me. They wanted to hear what I had to say. Abhay was there too, looking overwhelmed by everything they had done for us.

I quoted a Sanskrit *shloka* my grandfather had taught me when I was six years old: 'O God, I don't need a kingdom nor do I desire to be an emperor. I don't want rebirth or the golden vessels or heaven. I don't need anything from you. O Lord, if you want to give me something, then give me a soft heart and hard hands, so that I can wipe the tears of others.'

Silently, I came back to my chair. I didn't know what the women must be thinking or feeling at that moment.

An old devadasi climbed up on to the stage and stood there proudly. With a firm voice, she said, 'We want to give our akka a special gift. It is an embroidered bedspread and each of us has stitched some portion of it. So there are three thousand stitches. It may not look beautiful but we all wanted to be present in this bedspread.' Then she looked straight at me and continued, 'This is from our hearts to yours. This will keep you cool in the summer and warm in the winter—just like our affection towards you. You were by our side during our difficult times, and we want to be with you too.'

It is the best gift I have ever received.

2

How to Beat the Boys

Recently, when I visited the US, I had to speak to a crowd of both students and highly successful people. I always prefer interacting with the audience, so I opened the floor to questions.

After several questions were asked, a middle-aged man stood to speak. 'Ma'am, you are very confident and clear in communicating your thoughts. You are absolutely at ease while talking to us . . .'

I was direct. 'Please don't praise me. Ask me your question.'

'I think you must have studied abroad or done your MBA from a university in the West. Is that what gives you such confidence?' he asked.

Without wasting a second, I replied, 'It comes from my B.V.B.'

He seemed puzzled. 'What do you mean—my B.V.B.?'

I smiled. 'I'm talking about the Basappa Veerappa Bhoomaraddi College of Engineering and Technology in Hubli, a medium-sized town in the state of Karnataka in

India. I have never studied outside of India. The only reason I stand here before you is because of that college.'

In a lighter vein, I continued, 'I'm sure that the young people in the software industry who are present here today will appreciate the contribution of Infosys to India and to the US. Infosys has made Bengaluru, Karnataka and India proud. Had I not been in B.V.B., I would not have become an engineer. If I wasn't an engineer, then I wouldn't have been able to support my husband. And if my husband didn't have his family's backing, he may or may not have had the chance to establish Infosys at all! In that case, all of you wouldn't have gathered here today to hear me speak.'

Everyone clapped and laughed, but I really meant what I said. After the session got over and the crowd left, I felt tired and chose to sit alone on a couch nearby.

My mind went back to 1968. I was a seventeen-year-old girl with an abundance of courage, confidence and the dream to become an engineer. I came from an educated, though middle-class, conservative Brahmin family. My father was a professor of obstetrics and gynaecology in Karnataka Medical College at Hubli, while my mother was a schoolteacher before she got married.

I finished my pre-university exams with excellent marks and told my family that I wanted to pursue engineering. I had always been fascinated with science, even more so with its application. Engineering was one of those branches of science that would allow me to utilize my creativity, especially in design. But it was as if I had dropped a bomb inside our house.

The immediate reaction was of shock. Engineering was clearly an all-male domain and hence considered a taboo for girls in those days. There was no questioning the status quo, wherein girls were expected to be in the company of other female students in a medical or science college. The idea of a woman entering the engineering field had possibly never popped up in anyone's mind. It was akin to expecting pigs to fly.

I was my grandmother's favourite granddaughter, but even she looked at me with disdain and said, 'If you go ahead and do this, no man from north Karnataka will marry you. Who wants to marry a woman engineer? I am so disappointed in you.' My grandmother never thought that I would do anything she disapproved of. However, she also didn't know that in the city of Mysore, across the river of Tungabhadra, lived a man named Narayana Murthy who would later want to marry me.

My grandfather, a history teacher and my first guru to teach me reading and writing, only mildly opposed it. 'My child, you are wonderful at history. Why can't you do something in this field? You could be a great scholar one day. Don't chase a dry subject like engineering.'

My mother, who was extremely proficient in mathematics, said, 'You are good in maths. Why don't you complete your post-graduation in mathematics and get a job as a professor? You can easily work in a college after you get married instead of being a hard-core engineer struggling to balance family and work.'

My father, a liberal man who believed in education for women, thought for a moment and said, 'I think that you should pursue medicine. You are excellent with people and languages. To tell you the truth, I don't know much about engineering. We don't have a single engineer in our family. It is a male-dominated industry and you may not find another girl in your class. What if you have to spend four years without a real friend to talk to? Think about it. However, the decision is yours and I will support you.'

Many of my aunts also thought that no one would marry me if I chose engineering. This would possibly entail that I marry somebody from another community, an absolutely unheard of thing in those days.

However, I didn't care. As a student of history, I had read Hiuen Tsang's book *Si-Yu-Ki*. Before Tsang's travel to India, everybody discouraged him from making the journey on foot, but he refused to listen and decided to go. In time, he became famous for his seventeen-year-long journey to India. Taking courage from Tsang, I told my family, 'I want to do engineering. Come what may, I am ready for the consequences of my actions.'

I filled out the application form for B.V.B. College of Engineering and Technology, submitted it and soon received the news that I had been selected to the college on the basis of my marks. I was ecstatic, but little did I know that the college staff was discomfited by this development.

The principal at the time was B.C. Khanapure, who happened to know my father. They both met at a barber shop one day and the principal expressed his genuine anguish at what he perceived to be an awkward situation. He told my father, 'Doctor Sahib, I know that your daughter is very intelligent and that she has been given admission only because of merit, but I'm afraid we have some problems. She will be the only girl in college. It is going to be difficult for her. First, we don't have a ladies' toilet on campus. We don't have a ladies' room for her to relax either. Second, our boys are young with raging hormones and I am sure that they will trouble her. They may not do anything in front of the staff but they will definitely do something later. They may not cooperate with her or help her because they are not used to talking to girls. As a father of four daughters, I am concerned about yours too. Can you tell her to change her mind for her own sake?'

My father replied, 'I agree with you, Professor Sahib. I know you mean well, but my daughter is hell-bent on pursuing engineering. Frankly, she's not doing anything wrong. So I have decided to let her pursue it.'

'In that case, Doctor Sahib, I have a small request. Please ask her to wear a sari to college as it is a man's world out there and the sari will be an appropriate dress for the environment she will be in. She should not talk to the boys unnecessarily because that will give rise to rumours and that's never good for a girl in our society. Also, tell her to avoid going to the college canteen and spending time there with the boys.'

My father came back and told me about this conversation. I readily agreed to all of the requests since I had no intention of changing my mind.

Eventually, I would become friendly with some of the boys, but I always knew where to draw the line. The truth is that it were these same boys who would teach me some of life's lessons later, such as the value of keeping a sense of perspective, the importance of taking it easy every now and then and being a good sport. Many of the boys, who are now older gentlemen, are like my brothers even after fifty years! Finally, it was the lack of ladies' toilets on campus that made me understand the difficulty faced by many women in India due to the insufficiency or sheer absence of toilets. Eventually, this would lead me to build more than 13,000 toilets in Karnataka alone!

Meanwhile, my mother chose an auspicious day for me to pay the tuition fee. It was a Thursday and happened to be the end of the month. My mother nagged me to pay the fee of Rs 400 that day although my father only had Rs 300 left. He told her, 'Wait for a few days. I will get my salary and then Sudha can pay her fees.'

My mother refused to budge. 'Our daughter is going to college. It is a big deal. We must pay the fees today—it will be good for her studies.'

While they were still going back and forth, my father's assistant, Dr S.S. Hiremath, came along with his father-in-law, Patil, who was the headman of the Baad village near Shiggaon, the town where I was born. Patil curiously asked what was going on and my father explained the situation to him. He then took out his wallet and gave my father a hundred rupees. He said, 'Doctor Sahib, please accept this money. I want to gift it to this girl who is doing something path-breaking. I have seen parents take loans and sell their houses or farms to pay their sons' fees so that they can become engineers. In fact, sometimes, they don't even know whether their child will study properly or not. Look at your daughter. She desperately wants to do this and I think she is right.'

'No, Mr Patil,' my father refused. 'I can't take such an expensive gift. I will accept this as a loan and return it to you next month after I receive my salary.'

Patil continued as though he hadn't heard my father, 'The most important thing is for your daughter to do her best and complete her course and become a model for other girls.' Then he turned to me and said, 'Sudha, promise me that you will always be ethical, impartial and hard-working and that you will bring a good name to your family and society.'

I nodded meekly, suddenly humbled.

My first day of college arrived a month later. I wore a white sari for the first time, touched the feet of all the elders at home and prayed to Goddess Saraswati who had been very kind to me. I then made my way to the college.

As soon as I reached, the principal called me and gave me a key. He said, 'Here, Ms Kulkarni, take this. This is the key of a tiny room in the corner of the electrical engineering department on the second floor. You can use this room whenever you want.'

I thanked him profusely, took the key and immediately went to see the room. I opened the door excitedly, but alas! The room had two broken desks and there was no sign of a toilet. It was so dusty that I could not even consider entering it. Seeing me there, a cleaner came running with a broom in his hand. Without looking at me, he said, 'I'm so sorry. Principal Sahib told me yesterday that a girl student was going to join the college today, but I thought that he was joking. So I didn't clean the room. Anyway, I will do it right now.'

After he had finished cleaning, I still felt that the room was dusty. Calmly, I told him, 'Leave the broom here and give me a wet cloth, please. I will clean the room myself.'

After cleaning the room to my satisfaction, I brushed off the dust on my clothes and went to class.

When I entered the room on the ground floor, there were 149 pairs of eyes staring at me as though I were some kind of an exotic animal. It was true though. I was the one hundred and fiftieth animal in this zoo! I knew that some of them wanted to whistle but I kept a straight face and looked around for a place to sit. The first bench was empty. As I was about to sit there, I saw that someone had spilt blue ink right in the middle of the seat. This was obviously meant for me. I felt tears threatening to spill over, but I blinked them away. Making use of the newspaper in my hand, I wiped the seat clean and sat on a corner of the bench.

I could hear the boys whispering behind me. One grumbled, 'Why the hell did you put ink on the seat? Now she may go and complain to the principal.'

Another boy replied, 'How can she prove that I have done it? There are 149 of us here.'

Despite feeling hurt, I did not go to the principal to complain. He had already warned my father that if I complained, these boys might persist in troubling me further and I may eventually have to leave the college. So, I decided to keep quiet no matter how much these boys tried to harass me.

The truth was that I was afraid of being so troubled by the boys' activities that I would quit engineering altogether. I thought of ways to stay strong—physically and mentally. It would be my *tapas*, or penance. In that instant, I resolved that for the next four years, I would neither miss any class nor ask anyone for help with class notes. In an effort to teach myself self-restraint and self-control, I decided that until I completed my engineering degree, I would wear only white saris, refrain from sweets, sleep on a mat and take baths with cold water. I aimed to become self-sufficient; I would be my best friend and my worst enemy. I didn't know then that such a quote already existed in the Bhagavad Gita where Krishna says, '*Atma aiva hi atmano bandhu aatma aiva ripu atmanah*'.

We really don't need such penance to do well in our studies, but I was young and determined and wanted to do all I could to survive engineering.

I had good teachers who were considerate and sought to look out for me in class. They would occasionally ask, 'Ms Kulkarni, is everything okay with you?'

Even our college principal, Professor Khanapure, went out of his way to inquire about my welfare and if any boys were troubling me.

However, I can't say the same about my classmates.

One day, they brought a small bunch of flowers and stuck it in my plaited hair without my knowledge when the teacher was not around. I heard someone shout from the back—'Ms Flowerpot!' I quietly ran my fingers through my hair, found the flowers and threw them away. I did not say anything.

At times, they would throw paper airplanes at my back. Unfolding the papers, I would find comments such as, 'A woman's place is in the kitchen or in medical science or as a professor, definitely not in an engineering college.'

Others would read, 'We really pity you. Why are you performing penance like Goddess Parvati? At least Parvati had a reason for it. She wanted to marry Shiva. Who is your Shiva?' I would keep the paper planes and refrain from replying.

There was a famous student-friendly activity in our college known as 'fishpond'. Rather than an actual fishpond, it was a fish bowl that carried a collection of anonymous notes, or the 'fish'. Anybody from the college could write a comment or an opinion that would be read out later on our annual college day. All the students would eagerly wait to hear what funny and witty remarks had been selected that year. The designated host would stand on the stage in the college quadrangle and read the notes out loud. Every year, most of the notes were about me. I was often the target of Kannada limericks, one of which I can still remember vividly:

Avva avva genasa,
Kari seeri udisa,
Gandana manege kalisa.

This literally translates to:

> Mom Mom, there is a sweet potato,
> Please give me a black sari and send me to my
>   husband's house,
> This is because I'm always wearing a white sari.

Some of the romantic north Indian boys would modify the lyrics of songs from movies like *Teesri Kasam*:

> *Sajan re jhoot math bolo*
> *Sudha ke pass jaana hai*
> *Na haathi hai na ghoda hai*
> *Vahan paidal jaana hai.*

This can be translated as:

> Dear, come on, don't lie
> I want to go to Sudha
> I neither have an elephant nor a horse
> But I will go walking (to her).

All the boys would then sneak a glance at me to see my reaction, but I would simply hold back my tears and try my hardest to smile.

I knew that my classmates were acting out for a reason. It was not that they wanted to bully or harass me with deliberate intention as is the norm these days. It was just that they were unprepared—both mentally and physically—to deal with a person of the opposite sex studying with them. Our conservative society discouraged the mingling of boys and girls even as friends, and so, I was as interesting as an alien to them. My mind justified the reason for the boys' behaviour and helped me cope. And yet, the remarks, the pranks and the sarcasm continued to hurt.

My only outlet in college was my actual education. I enjoyed the engineering subjects and did very well in my exams. I found that I performed better than the boys, even in hard-core engineering subjects such as smithy, filing, carpentry and welding. The boys wore blue overalls and I wore a blue apron over my sari. I knew that I looked quite funny, but it was a small price to pay for the education I was getting.

When the exam results were announced, everyone else knew my marks before I did. Almost every semester, my classmates and seniors would make a singular effort to find out my marks and display them on the notice board for everyone to see. I had absolutely no privacy.

Over the course of my studies, I realized that the belief 'engineering is a man's domain' is a complete myth. Not only was I just as capable as them, I also scored higher than all my classmates. This gave me additional confidence and I continued to not miss a single day or a single class. I persisted in studying hard, determined to top the subsequent examinations. In time, I became unfazed that my marks were displayed on the notice board. On the contrary, I was proud that I was beating all the boys at their own game as I kept bagging the first rank in the university.

My ability to be self-sufficient made me strong and the boys eventually started to respect me, became dependent on me for surveys and drawings and asked me for the answers of the assignments. I began to make friends and even today, my good friends include Ramesh Jangal from the civil department, my lab partner Sunil Kulkarni, and Fakeer Gowda, M.M. Kulkarni, Hire Gowda, Anand Uthuri, Gajanan Thakur, Prakash Padaki, H.P. Sudarshan and Ramesh Lodaya.

I will never forget my teachers: L.J. Noronha from the electrical engineering department, Yoga Narasimha, a gifted teacher from Bengaluru, Prof. Mallapur from the chemistry department, Prof. Kulkarni from hydraulics and many more. Between my classes, I also spent much time in the library and the librarian became very fond of me over time, eventually giving me extra books.

I also spoke frequently to the gardener about the trees that should be planted in front of the college, and during my four years there, I had him plant coconut trees. Whenever I go to B.V.B. now, I look at the coconut trees and fondly remember my golden days on the campus.

The four years passed quickly and the day came when I finally had to leave. I felt sad. I had come as a scared teenager and was leaving as a confident and bright young engineer! College had taught me the resilience to face any situation, the flexibility to adjust as needed, the importance of building good and healthy relationships with others, sharing notes with classmates and collaborating with others instead of staying by myself. Thus, when I speak of friends, I don't usually think of women but rather of men because I really grew up with them. When I later entered the corporate world, it was again dominated by men. It was only natural for my colleague or friend to be a man and only sometimes would there be women, whom I have got to know over many years.

College is not just a building made up of walls, benches and desks. It is much more intangible than that. The right education should make you a confident person and that is what B.V.B. did for me.

I later completed my master's programme from the Indian Institute of Science, Bengaluru. Yet, B.V.B. continues to have a special place in my heart.

When my father passed away due to old age, I decided to do something in his memory. He had allowed me to go ahead and become an engineer, despite all the odds and the grievances he had heard from our family and society. Thus, I built a lecture hall in his memory in our college campus.

Whenever I go abroad to deliver a speech, at least five people of different ages come and tell me that they are from B.V.B, too. I connect with them immediately and can't help but smile and ask, 'Which year did you graduate? Who were your teachers? How many girls studied in your class?'

Now, whenever I go back to the college, it is like a celebration, like a daughter coming home. Towards the end of the visit, I almost always stand alone in the inner quadrangle of the stage. My memories take me back to the numerous occasions when I received awards for academic excellence. I then spend a few minutes in front of the notice board and walk up to the small room on the second floor of the electrical engineering department that was 'Kulkarni's Room', but no longer dusty now. I remember the bench on which I sat and prepared for my exams. My heart feels a familiar ache when I recall some of my teachers and classmates who are no longer in this world today.

And then, as I walk down the stairs, I come across groups of girls—chatting away happily and wearing jeans, skirts or traditional salwar kameezes. There are almost as many girls as there are boys in the college. When they see me, they lovingly surround me for autographs. In the midst of the crowd and the signings, I think of my parents and my journey of fifty years and my eyes get misty.

May God bless our college, B.V.B!

3

Food for Thought

Rekha is a very dear friend and our families have known each other for generations. Since I hadn't seen her for a long time, I decided to visit her. I picked up the phone and dialled her number.

Her father, Rao, who is like a father to me, picked up the phone. 'Hello?'

We exchanged greetings and I said, 'Uncle, I am coming to your house for lunch tomorrow.'

Her father, a botanist, was very happy. 'Please do. Tomorrow is a Sunday and we can relax a little bit. Don't run off quickly!' he replied.

In a city such as Bengaluru, going from Jayanagar to Malleswaram on a weekday usually takes a minimum of two hours. Travelling on a Sunday is much easier because it takes only half the time. When I reached her home the next day, I could smell that lunch was almost ready, and yet the aromas wafting in from the kitchen indicated to me that the day's menu would somehow be different. None of the typical Karnataka dishes were laid out on the table, and the cuisine was, in fact, quite bland for my taste.

'I may wear a simple sari but I am a foodie, Rekha! Is the lunch specially arranged so that I don't come again?' I joked, as one can with an old friend who will not misunderstand and take offence.

Rekha's father laughed heartily. 'Well,' he sighed. 'Today is my mother's *shraddha* or death anniversary. On this day, we always prepare a meal from indigenous vegetables.'

'What do you mean by indigenous?' I was perplexed. 'Aren't all the vegetables available in our country indigenous, except perhaps ones like cauliflower, cabbage and potato?'

'Oh my God! You have just begun a wrong topic on a wrong day with the wrong person!' exclaimed Rekha in mock dismay. 'After lunch, I think I should just leave you with my father and join you both later in the evening. This will take at least four hours of your time.'

I knew that Rekha's father was a botanist, but it was then that I realized that he was passionate about this subject. Though I had known him for a really long time, I had never seen this facet of his personality before. Probably, he had been too busy during his working years while we had been too busy playing and fooling around.

'Is this really true, Uncle?' I asked.

He nodded.

Since I come from a farmer's family on my paternal side, I have always had a fascination for vegetables. I knew vaguely about the things we could grow, the seasons to grow them in and the ones that we could not grow, including the reasons why.

However, whenever I broached the subject with friends interested in agriculture and farming, I never really received a proper answer. Finally, here was a man more than willing to share his knowledge with me! I couldn't resist.

'You know, Rekha,' I said, 'it is difficult to get knowledgeable people to spend time explaining their subject matter to others. Today, Google is like my grandmother. I log on to the website any time I require an explanation of something I don't understand or want to learn about.'

'Right now, you are logging on to an encyclopaedia,' Rekha smiled and glanced at her father affectionately.

The conversation drifted to other subjects as we ate lunch. The meal constituted of rice, sambar without chillies, daal with black pepper and not chillies, gorikayi (cluster beans), methi saag, cucumber raita and rice payasam. It was accompanied by udin vada with black pepper. There was pickle and some plain yogurt on the side too. After we had eaten this lunch well-suited for someone recovering in a hospital, Rekha's father said, 'Come, let's go to the garden.'

Rekha's family owned an old house in the corner of a street. Her grandfather had been in the British railways and was lucky enough to buy the corner plot at a low price and had built a small home with a large garden there. In a city like Bengaluru, filled with apartments and small spaces, the garden was something of a privilege and a luxury.

Uncle and I walked to the garden while Rekha took a nap. He settled himself on a bench, while I looked around. It was a miniature forest with a large kitchen garden of carrots, okra, fenugreek and spinach—each segregated neatly into sections. A few sugar canes shone brightly in front of us while a dwarf papaya tree heavy with fruit stood in a corner. On the other end was a line of maize as well as flowering trees such as the *parijata* (the Indian coral tree), and roses of varying colours.

'Uncle and Aunty must be spending a lot of time here making this place beautiful,' I thought. 'All the trees and plants seem healthy—almost as if they are happy to be here!'

'Do you think that all the vegetables we have around us are from India? Or are they from other countries?' he asked out of the blue.

I felt as if I was back in school in front of my teacher. But I wasn't scared. Even if I gave him a wrong answer, it wasn't going to affect my progress report. 'Of course, Uncle! India has the largest population of vegetarians. So, in time, we have learnt to make different kinds of vegetarian dishes. Even people who eat meat avoid it during traditional events such as festivals, weddings, death anniversaries and the month of *Shravana*.'

'I agree with your assessment of everything, except that most vegetables are grown in India. The truth is that the majority of our vegetables are not ours at all. They have come from different countries.'

I stared at him in disbelief.

He pointed to a tomato plant—a creeper with multiple fruits, tied to a firm bamboo stick. 'Look at this! Is this an Indian vegetable?'

I thought of tomato soup, tomato rasam, tomato bhat (tomato-flavoured rice), sandwiches and chutney.

'Of course it is. We use it every single day. It is an integral part of Indian cuisine.'

Uncle smiled. 'Well, the tomato did not originate in India, but in Mexico. It made its way to Europe in 1554. Since nobody ate tomatoes over there at the time, they became ornamental plants because of the beautiful deep-red colour. At some point, there was a belief in Europe that it was good for curing infertility, while some thought that it was poisonous. The contradicting perspectives made it difficult for this fruit to be incorporated into their diet for a long time. Its lack of value must have been a real push for initiating Spain's tomato festival, where millions of tomatoes are used every year to this day. A story goes that one business-savvy European surrounded his tomato plants with a sturdy, thick fence to show his neighbours that the fruits were not poisonous, but rather valuable and thus desirable. Gradually, the fruits reached India and began to be used as a commercial crop, thanks to its tempting colour and taste. It must have come to us during the reign of the British. But today, we cannot think of cooking without tomatoes.'

'Wow!' I thought. Out loud, I said, 'Uncle, tell me about an essential item that is used in our cooking but isn't ours.'

'Come on, try and guess. We simply cannot cook without this particular vegetable.'

I closed my eyes and thought of sambar, that essential south Indian dish and the mutter paneer typical of the north Indian cuisine. It took me a while to think of a common ingredient—the chilli. I brushed my thought away. 'No, there's no way that the chilli can be an imported vegetable. There can be no Indian food without it,' I thought.

Uncle looked at me. 'You are right. It is the chilli!' he exclaimed almost as if he had read my mind.

'How did you know?'

'Because people never fail to be shocked when they think of the possibility that chilli could be from another country. I can see it clearly on their faces when the wheels turn inside their head.'

My disbelief was obvious. How could we cook without chillies? It is as important as salt in Indian cooking.

'There are many stories and multiple theories about chillies,' Uncle said. 'When Vasco da Gama came to India, he came from Portugal via Brazil and brought many seeds with him. Later, Marco Polo and the British came to India. Thus, many more plant seeds arrived. The truth is that what we call "indigenous" isn't really ours. Think of chillies, capsicum, corn, groundnut, cashews, beans, potato, papaya, pineapple, custard apple, guava and sapodilla—they are all from South America. Over time, we indigenized them and learnt how to cook them. Some say that the chilli came from the country of the same name, while some others say it came from Mexico. According to a theory, black pepper was the ingredient traditionally used in India to make our food hot and spicy. Some scholars believe that the sole goal of the East India Company was to acquire a monopoly over India's pepper trade, which later ended in India's colonization. But when we began using chillies, we found that it tasted better than black pepper.

To give you an example, we refer to black pepper as *kalu menasu* in Kannada. We gave a similar name to the chilli and called it *menasin kai*. In Hindi, it is frequently referred to as *mirchi*. In the war between black pepper and chilli, the former lost and chilli established itself as the new prince and continues to rule the Indian food industry even today. north Karnataka is famous for its red chillies now.'

'That much I do know, Uncle!' I closed my eyes and had a vision of my younger days. 'I remember seeing acres and acres of red chilli plants during my childhood. The harvest used to take place during the Diwali season. I remember that the Badgi district was dedicated to the sale of chillies. I had gone with my uncle one day and was amazed by the mountains of red chillies I saw there.'

'Oh yes, you are right! Those red chillies are bright red in colour but they aren't really hot or spicy. On the contrary, chillies that grow in the state of Andhra Pradesh in the area of Guntur are extremely spicy. They are a little rounded in shape, not as deep red in colour and are called Guntur chillies. A good cook uses a combination of different kinds of chillies to make the dish delicious and attractive. Now that's what I call indigenous.'

'There were also two other kinds of chillies in our farm— one was a chilli called Gandhar or Ravana chilli that grows upside down and the other one, of course, was capsicum.'

Uncle nodded. 'Capsicum in India is nothing but green or red bell peppers in the West. But if you eat one tiny Ravana chilli, you will have to sit in the bathroom with your backside in pain and drink many bottles of water for a long,

long time! Or you will have to eat five hundred grams of candies, sweets or chocolates.'

We both laughed.

Hearing the laughter, Rekha's mother came and joined us. 'Are you folks joking about today's menu? I'm sorry that there wasn't much variety. When I heard that you were coming for lunch, I told Uncle to inform you that today's food was going to be bland and that you could come another Sunday, but he said that you are like family and wouldn't mind at all,' she said to me.

That sparked my interest. 'Tell me the reason for the bland food, Aunty!'

'We have a method to the madness, I guess. During death anniversaries, we do not use vegetables or spices that have come from other countries. Hence, we use ingredients like fenugreek, black pepper and cucumber, among others. Our ancestors were scared of using new vegetables and named these imports Vishwamitra *srishti*.'

This was the first time that I had heard of such a thing. 'What does that mean?'

Aunty settled into a makeshift chair under the guava tree. 'The story goes that there was a king called Trishanku who wanted to go to heaven along with his physical body. With his strong penance and powers, the sage Vishwamitra was able to send him to heaven, but the gods pushed him back because they were worried that it would set a precedent for people to come in with their physical bodies. That was not to be allowed. Vishwamitra tried to push Trishanku upwards but the gods pushed him down, like a game of tug of war. In the end, Vishwamitra created a new world for Trishanku and called it Trishanku Swarga. He even created vegetables that belonged neither to the earth nor heaven. So vegetables like eggplant and cauliflower are the creations of Vishwamitra, which must not be used at a time such as a dear one's death anniversary.'

Silence fell between us and I pondered over Aunty's story. After a few minutes, I saw Rekha coming towards us with some bananas and oranges and a box of what seemed to be dessert.

'Come,' she said to me, 'have something. The banana is from our garden and the dessert is made from home-grown ingredients too! You must be . . .'

Uncle interrupted, 'Do you know that we make so many desserts in India that aren't original to our country?'

'Appa, tell her the story of the guava and the banana. I really like that one,' Rekha said. She smiled as she handed me a banana.

Uncle grinned, pleased to impart some more knowledge. 'The seeds of guava came from Goa,' he said. 'So some people say that's how it was named. In Kannada, we call it *perala hannu* because we believe that it originated in Peru, South America. Let me tell you a story.

'Durvasa was a famed short-tempered sage in our ancient epics. He cursed anyone who dared to rouse his anger. The sage was married to a woman named Kandali. One day, she said to him, "O sage, people are terribly afraid of you while I have lived with you for such a long time. Don't you think I deserve a great boon from you?"

'Though Durvasa was upset at her words, he did not curse her. He thought seriously about what she had said and decided that she was right. "I will give you a boon. But only one. So think carefully," he said.

'After some thought, she replied, "Create a fruit for me that is unique and blessed with beautiful colours. The tree should grow not in heaven but on earth. It should have the ability to grow easily everywhere in our country. It must give fruits in bunches and for the whole year. The fruit must not have any seeds and must not create a mess when we eat it. When it is not ripe, we should be able to use it as a vegetable and once it is ripe, we should use it while performing pujas. We must be able to use all parts of the tree."

'Durvasa was surprised and impressed at the number of specifications his wife was giving him. He was used to giving curses in anger and then figuring out their solutions once he had calmed down, but this seemingly simple request was a test of his intelligence. "No wonder women are cleverer. Men like me get upset quickly and act before fully thinking of the consequences," he thought.

'The sage prayed to Goddess Saraswati to give him the knowledge with which he could satisfy his wife's demand. After a few minutes, he realized that he would be able to fulfil his wife's desire. Thus he created the banana tree, which is found all over India today. Every part of the tree—the leaf, the bark, the stem, the flowers and its fruits are used daily. Raw banana can be cooked while the ripe banana can be eaten easily by peeling off its skin. It is also an essential part of worship to the gods. The fruit is seedless and presents itself as a bunch. A mature tree lives for a year and smaller saplings are found around it.

'Kandali was ecstatic and named the plant *kandari*. She announced, "Whoever eats this fruit will not get upset, despite the fact that it was created by my short-tempered husband."

'Over a period of time, people started using the banana extensively and loved it. Slowly the name kandari changed to *kadali* and the banana came to be known as kadali *phala* in Sanskrit.' Uncle took a deep breath at the end of his story.

I smiled, amused at the story that seemed to result from fertile imagination. I had a strong urge to grab a banana and took one from the plate in front of me. 'You may have given me bland food today,' I said, 'but I really want some dessert.'

Rekha opened the box. It was filled with different varieties of sweets. I saw gulab jamuns, jhangri (a deep-fried flour-based dessert) and gulkhand (a rose petal-based preserve). I can't resist gulab jamuns, so I immediately picked one up and popped it into my drooling mouth. It was soft and sweet. 'What a dessert!' I remarked, amazed at how delicious it was! 'Nobody can beat us when it comes to Indian desserts. I don't know how people can live in other countries without gulab jamuns.'

'Wait a minute, don't make such sweeping statements,' said Rekha. 'Gulab jamun is not from India.'

'Yeah, right,' I said, not convinced at all. Before she could stop me, I grabbed another gulab jamun and gulped it down.

'I'm serious. A language scholar once came to speak in our college. He told us that apart from English, we use multiple Persian, Arabic and Portuguese words that we aren't even aware of. Gulab jamun is a Persian word and is a dish prepared in Iran. It became popular in India during the Mughal reign because the court language was Persian. The same is true for jhangri, which is a kind of ornament worn on the wrist and the jhangri design resembles it.'

'You will now tell me that even gulkhand is from somewhere else!' I complained loudly.

She grinned, 'You aren't wrong! Gulkhand is a Persian word too—*gul* is nothing but rose and *khand* means sweet. Gul, in fact, originates from the word *gulab* (rose).'

My brain was thoroughly exhausted with all this information. When I saw the oranges, I said with pride, 'I will not call this an orange now, but its Kannada name *narangi*.'

Uncle cleared his throat. 'Narangi is an Indian word but it does not originate in Karnataka. It is made up of two words—*naar* (orange or colour of the sun) and *rangi* (colour).'

The conversation was leaving me feeling truly lost.

'When people stay in one place for some time,' he continued, 'they will unknowingly absorb the culture around them, including their food and language. At times, we adopt the changes into our local cuisine and make it our own. That's exactly what happened with the foods we have discussed.'

I glanced at my watch. It was time for me to leave. I thanked them profusely, especially Uncle, for enlightening me in a way that even Google could not.

There was a huge traffic jam despite it being a Sunday evening as I set out for home, but I wasn't bored on the way. In fact, I was happy to recollect Uncle's words and perhaps, as a result, suddenly remembered an incident.

My mother had two sisters. Though all three sisters were married to men from the same state, their husbands' jobs were in different areas—one lived in south Karnataka in the old Mysore state, my parents lived in Maharashtra and the third stayed in the flatlands in a remote corner of Karnataka.

After their husbands retired, the three sisters lived in Hubli in the same area. It was fun to meet my cousins every day and eat meals together. We celebrated festivals as a family and the food was cooked in one house, though everybody brought home-cooked desserts from their own houses.

During one particular Diwali, we had a host of delicacies. My mother made puri and shrikhand (a popular dish in Maharashtra made from strained yogurt and sugar). My aunt from Mysore made kishmish kheer and a rice-based main course called bisi bele anna, while the other aunt made groundnut-based sweets such as jaggery-based sticky chikki and ball-shaped laddus.

As children, my cousins and I had plenty of fun eating them but in the car, I realized for the first time that all the sisters had absorbed something from the area that they had lived in. Despite their physical proximity, the food in each household was so diverse. I couldn't help but wonder how exciting the food really must be in the different regions of India.

I thought of paneer pizzas, cheese dosas and the Indian 'Chinese' food. They must have originated the same way.

Who really said that India is a country? It is a continent—culturally vibrant, diverse in food and yet, distinctly Indian at heart.

4

Three Handfuls of Water

When I was young, I lived with my grandparents in a tiny village in Karnataka.

My grandmother, Krishnakka, was a good-looking lady. But I rarely saw her dress well, unless there was a festival or an important event.

When I came back from school one day, I found her just about to open a big wooden box containing her silk saris and a few dear possessions. Since she rarely opened this particular box, it always carried an air of fascination for me. I'd always drop whatever I was doing to join her. This time was no different. I dropped my bag and ran to her. I peeped inside and saw a silver kumkum *bharani* (a box used to keep the red powder used for social or religious purposes), a small mirror with a silver handle, a broken, yet useful ivory comb and a few silver vessels.

'My father gave these to me on my wedding,' said my grandmother with pride in her voice. Her father had been gone a long time.

I took the kumkum box in my hand and stared at it. It was a round-shaped box that looked like a miniature pagoda.

I removed the cover and opened it without a second thought. There were three parts to it—the first one contained honeybee wax, the second was a small round mirror and at the bottom was a space to keep the kumkum. I was fascinated. 'Avva,' I began, a little hesitant. 'Out of all your gifts, I love the kumkum bharani the most. Will you please give this to me when I grow up?'

'I have thirteen grandchildren. Each of them must get something. But I will keep this for you,' she smiled as she replied candidly.

Later, she sat unhurriedly in front of a full-length mirror, brushed her hair, wore a nose ring and a nine-yard green Banarasi sari with a yellow blouse. She put on a big bindi and pretty pearl earrings, and decorated her hands with green glass bangles and two gold ones. Then she circled her bun with flowers. She perfectly fit the image of an elderly woman from north Karnataka.

'Avva, there is no festival today. Why are you dressed up like this? Are you going somewhere?' I asked.

'I am going out for lunch and you are going to come with me. Get ready quickly.'

When I paused for a few moments, she added, 'Don't worry about your afternoon class. Your teacher is also coming there.'

In the village school, this kind of adjustment was not unusual. Sometimes, we got a day off in the middle of the week and it was compensated for on a Sunday. Things were more fluid and life was simple, and I was but a bud flowering in this forest of my own.

I didn't need to be told a second time. I was happy at the thought of attending a lunch party and ran to change my clothes. Even in those days, I never took more than a few minutes to get ready.

Avva wasn't usually a talkative person, but she was in a good mood that day. As my grandfather wasn't inclined to accompany her for such functions, she told her husband, 'I am going out for lunch to Indira's house today. I have kept your meal covered with a plantain leaf. Please have it as soon as possible.'

My grandfather, whom I affectionately called Shiggaon Kaka, nodded and continued reading the newspaper.

Within minutes, we stepped out and started walking towards Indira Ajji's house.

'What's the occasion?' I asked.

'My friend Indira has come back from Varanasi and has invited all of us for lunch. It is a wonderful celebration called Kashi Samaradhane.'

'What is that? If Indira Ajji has returned from a visit, then why do we have to celebrate it? Isn't it like going to Hubli or Gadag and coming back? We don't have any party or celebration then!'

Avva sighed. 'There is a lot of difference between going to Kashi and going to Hubli. Kashi is one of the most sacred places on earth. The river Ganga flows there. It is believed that Lord Vishwanath, the Lord of the universe, resides there and gives boons to everyone. It is his favourite place on the planet. There are eighty ghats to bathe in there. Thousands of Sanskrit scholars live in the city. The sari that I am wearing today is known as a Banarasi sari. If you get such a sari as a wedding gift, it is considered to be very lucky as it is from the holy land of Kashi.'

I wasn't fully convinced. 'Still, why is such a lunch organized?' I persisted, despite my desperate desire to eat the goodies at the celebration anyway.

'It is not easy to go to Kashi, no matter how rich or devoted you are. Going there and coming back is an arduous journey. You have to switch many trains and buses. First, people there speak a different language called Hindi. Second, we don't have any relatives to lean on or direct us. Third, it is so cold during winter that you can't even submerge your feet in the freezing river. Fourth, in the summer, the heat makes the ground so flaming hot that you can't walk barefoot for the pujas. Fifth, if the locals there find out that we are outsiders, then more often than not, they try to cheat us. There are stories of people going to Kashi without ever coming back. So when someone returns, we consider them blessed. That's why they give us a feast and we exchange gifts.'

'What are you going to give, Avva?' I was curious.

Avva opened the bag that she was carrying. There was a nice cotton sari inside, along with plenty of fruits and flowers.

'And what will she give us?'

'We will get a Kashi thread and some water from the Ganga, both of which are precious. Wear the thread on your wrist or your neck every day and God will protect you from difficulties.'

That was good news indeed. I needed all the protection I could get for my upcoming examinations.

'You are lucky to get it at such a young age,' Avva said, as she incorrectly interpreted the reason for my smile.

'What does the Kashi thread look like?'

'Well, it is a simple knotted black thread. Kashi is protected by Bhairavnath, who is a great and loyal servant of Lord Shiva. If you go to Kashi and don't see the Kaal Bhairav temple, your yatra or journey is considered incomplete. You will get a Kashi thread from there, which you have to wear for Bhairavnath to protect you. Since the Kashi trip is difficult, he will accompany you in his invisible form until you reach home safely. Then he runs back to assist the next devotee,' finished my grandmother.

'Hmm,' I thought. 'What if he has to help more than one person home?'

Before I could ask, Avva answered, 'I know what you are going to ask me now. Bhairavnath can multiply himself as many times as he wants to.'

So instead, I asked, 'What is the use of the water from the Ganga?'

'Silly girl, how can I ever describe the use of the holy water?' She patted my head affectionately. 'The Ganga is the life of our country. Everybody wants to drink the holy water, but it isn't possible for people like us who live in south India. So we keep a few spoons of *Gangajal*, the holy water from the Ganga, for whoever is in the last days of their life so that they can go to heaven.'

'Avva,' I asked, 'if Kashi is so important and you believe in it so much, then Kaka and you must go there. I will also come with you.'

Avva turned thoughtful. 'I have never ventured out of Karnataka,' she said. 'You know that Kaka and I avoid eating anything when we travel. It takes at least ten days to go to Kashi. And it's better to travel in a group because we don't know the local language. It is difficult to form such a group here, and we are also getting old. We don't want to fall sick on the way and burden the group. So going to Kashi will most likely remain a dream for me. But I am happy that Indira has gone there with her cousins. At least I can visit her and listen to her stories.'

At the time, I didn't understand why my grandmother had such devotion for this holy land.

Soon, we reached Indira Ajji's house. The whole atmosphere was festive. Stumps of banana trees and mango leaves were tied to the sides of the gate. There were plenty of flower decorations all over the place. An intricate rangoli design was drawn on the floor at the entrance. I immediately spotted my classmates running here and there with glee. My teacher was offering home-made drinks to all the children. On one side lay fifty pots containing Gangajal. All the pots had black threads tied around the neck. They were piled up on a table decorated with flowers. A single banana leaf was laid out nearby with all the dishes, though there was no one sitting there. My mind raced to count the number of desserts on the leaf.

Avva and I entered the main room. Since my grandmother was the oldest person there and quite popular too, people seemed to be happy to see her. Avva turned to Indira, 'You are so lucky to have visited Kashi, bathed in the river Ganga and seen Lord Vishwanath in all his glory.'

Indira Ajji smiled gently and invited both of us to sit down. People were gathered around her to hear more about her trip.

Somebody asked, 'What did you think of the famous Annapoorna temple?'

'It was beautiful,' she replied. 'It is located before Lord Vishwanath's temple and is the only temple where Shiva is believed to ask for alms and food from his wife with his begging bowl. He is said to appear in the temple only on a few special days.'

As people started asking more questions, I became bored.

Slowly, I nudged my grandmother. When she turned to look at me, I pointed to the banana leaf and asked, 'Avva, why is nobody sitting for lunch there? I am hungry. Can I go eat the food?'

'Don't even think about it! That food is for Bhairavnath. He has much work to do and has to make the trip back soon. But you can pray to him if you want.'

I didn't see anyone sitting there but remembered that he was supposed to be invisible. So I joined my hands together and prayed facing the leaf.

A short while later, we all had a delicious lunch.

On our way back, my grandmother remarked, 'Isn't it wonderful to hear that Indira took three handfuls of water from the river Ganga and saluted the rising sun? It must be such a beautiful sight. Sometimes, I also wish to do the same. I have convinced myself that the rivulet in our garden is also another form of the Ganga and if I worship her, it is as good as worshipping the river in Kashi.'

It was evening by the time we reached home and from a distance, I could see my grandfather sitting in the verandah. Kaka was my good friend and I ran to tell him about the day.

Just as I approached him, he smiled and asked, 'Did your grandmother tell you about what you must leave behind in Kashi?'

'What are you talking about, Kaka?'

'In the olden days, the journey to Kashi took months and not days. Today, we have trains and roads but then people had to walk and cross forests and face dangers on their way. Many did not make it back to their homes. Emperor Akbar abolished the jizya tax for entry into Varanasi whereas Aurangzeb reintroduced it. Hence the journey to Kashi was expensive. If someone made it to Kashi successfully, they would make an unusual vow—to give up whatever they loved the most after taking three handfuls of water, keeping Lord Sun as a witness. A word given to the Ganga in such a way is considered unbreakable and one is obliged to fulfil it.'

I was fascinated and waited as Kaka took a deep breath.

'There are certain rules that you must follow.'

'What rules?'

'One cannot give up eating rice, wheat flour, milk, lentils, ghee or jaggery. One can give up eating one vegetable and one fruit that freely grows around their hometown or area and a dessert that they love. So if you love jalebis, you can vow to abstain from it, but you can't give up something that you don't like, such as bitter gourd. Whenever you see what you have given up, it will remind you of Kashi.'

'That is quite tough, Kaka!'

My grandfather continued as if he hadn't heard me, 'If a husband and wife go together, they can choose to give up the same things. That is easy as it means that they won't have to cook separately. But if a husband and wife visit individually and choose to abstain from different things, then both of them must leave whatever the other has, too.'

Avva, meanwhile, reached the verandah.

'That sounds too complicated!' I thought. Out loud, I asked, 'Is it very hard to leave what you like, Kaka?'

'It depends on the individual. If you decide to fulfil your vow with your heart and soul, then the desire for the object goes away with time and that way of life simply becomes a habit.'

'What will you leave if you go to Kashi?' I asked mischievously.

'I love your Avva and that's why I will never go to Kashi!' he replied with a twinkle in his eye.

Though Avva was old, she suddenly became shy and quickly walked in.

In a more serious tone, he added, 'It is not up to us to go there. It is Lord Vishwanath's wish. He will call us when it's our time.'

Years flew by and seasons went past. Avva died without ever going to Kashi. She passed away on the day she always wanted to—the day of Bhishmastami or the day Bhishma died. It is believed that the gates of heaven are open on this day. I was in Pune then and by the time I reached Hubli, I could only see her ashes and her picture on the wall. My memory of Avva remained that of an active, cheerful, helpful and affectionate woman.

Based on Avva's last instructions, my aunt gave me the kumkum box and I preserved it like a treasure in an old chest, but did not use it as often as she did because by then, sticker bindis had invaded the Indian market.

As time went by, I started reading extensively and became completely fascinated with Buddhism. Buddha's compassionate heart moved me in ways that I cannot express and I understood why he had taken the famous middle path. Buddhism is represented by a wheel and two deer. Sarnath, the place that had played a big role in Buddha's life and was the place of his first sermon, was a deer park located only a few kilometres away from Varanasi. I realized then that the city got its name from the rivers Varuna and Assi that both join the river Ganga at this location. It is believed to be a sacred land since time immemorial.

In 629 AD, when the Chinese traveller Hiuen Tsang visited India, he described Varanasi in great detail along with a description of its temples, rivulets and the richness of the surroundings. I felt an increasing desire to go to Kashi and yet, it somehow became low on my list of priorities because of work and routine.

During the festival of Diwali in 1995, I received a gift in the form of a book called *Banaras: City of Light* by Diana L. Eck.

I kept it aside, intending to read it after the wonderful madness of the festival was over.

That year, our family decided to celebrate with a traditional *aarti*. I went to my bedroom and opened the old chest. I began rummaging through it to find the silver plate for the puja. Suddenly, I saw the kumkum box. It was a strong reminder of Avva and I forgot about the plate. Gently, I took out the box and recalled the way she used to wear her kumkum. I saw her dressing up for Kashi Samaradhane and remembered how we had walked for the lunch together. Oh, how I used to pester her to give me the treasured kumkum bharani! She believed wholeheartedly in the holiness of Kashi but never visited the city or regretted the miss! I thought to myself, 'Going to Kashi is not tough now. Moreover, I have Diana's book with me. It will help me understand the city better before I go. Maybe I should do it for the sake of my grandmother . . .'

'Are you meditating in there?' my mom called out, cutting my thoughts short. 'Everyone is waiting.'

I found the silver plate quickly and gave it to my mother along with the kumkum bharani.

'Good, this is my mother's precious possession. It will be as if her spirit is with us during the prayers today,' she said.

Once the festive season had ended, I began reading Diana's book—a masterpiece in itself. It was, in fact, the author's PhD thesis at Harvard. She, a foreigner, had come to India and stayed here for years studying about the religious places in our country. And here I was, doing nothing! I felt ashamed of myself. The book inspired me to get to Kashi as soon as I could, if only to satisfy my childhood curiosity and my grandmother's desire.

In February 1996, I managed to find my way there all by myself. I stayed in a hotel and had the darshan of Lord Vishwanath, whose temple was in a corner of the city. He was worshipped using the three-leaved Bilva (Lord Shiva's tree) *patras* and constantly bathed by his devotees who gathered there. There were security gunmen, a barbed wire fence and the Gyanvapi mosque near the temple. The different image of the place I had in my mind disappointed me a little, but I was amazed by the faith of the people of varied ages who had come from all over the country.

Once that was done, I went to see the Manikarnika ghat, where dead bodies are cremated every day and almost endlessly. The strong belief that dying in Kashi is a gateway to heaven has not changed even with the increase in literacy and the changing culture. I visited some more ghats and was taken aback by the amount of dirt in this holy city. I also visited the Banaras Hindu University that was established single-handedly by Madan Mohan Malaviya, and beautiful museums depicting Hindustani ragas through enchanting paintings.

I walked to numerous temples, small and big, including the temples of Annapoorna Devi, Bhairavnath and the famous Hanuman temple named Sankat Mochan, where the monkeys outnumbered the devotees. Though plenty of black threads were being sold around me, I didn't buy any because I had grown out of the belief.

The holy Ganga water was abundant and up for sale in different volumes, shapes and sizes. Even today, the water is considered holy.

In the small lanes of Kashi, I wandered around, aimless and happy in the moment. The beautiful views and the pretty saris caught my eye. What a gorgeous invention the sari is—a rare combination of the cloth-tying method of the Greeks, the Romans and our own. Whenever I travel abroad, I come across people who are fascinated with the border, the richness, the zari and the pallu, which automatically bestows a royal appearance to whoever wears it.

Kashi boasts of unique Banarasi saris which have changed over the years but still remain attractive. I planned to buy a few saris for myself—a pastel-coloured one, a bright one suitable for evening wear and a dark green sari like the one Avva had. The sellers called out to me and the other passers-by. I absolutely loved shopping for saris. But then I changed my mind. 'What was the hurry? I will shop tomorrow after I have seen more,' I thought. So I went about doing some window shopping.

Then I went back to the ghats and finally reached the busy Dashashwamedh ghat. The crowd was preparing for the evening aarti. I glanced at the tourists—they seemed to come not just from different states but also from different countries. They were smiling and taking pictures of their surroundings. The dirt, the small lanes and the claustrophobic closeness of it all did not seem to bother them. The sadhus were in half-meditation and most of the devotees were preparing for their dip in the water. I was tempted. 'Why can't I bathe in the

Ganga too? Maybe I can also offer three handfuls of water to the Ganga and complete my Kashi experience.'

I looked around and the dirt suddenly gave me second thoughts. I didn't want to take a dip there. As if it was meant to be, I remembered an old friend Ajay who lived near the Gai ghat. Maybe I could ask him if there was a cleaner and less crowded spot more suitable for me.

So I located a landline nearby and phoned him. It was obvious that Ajay was upset because I hadn't informed him of my visit. He gave me strict instructions to remain where I was and within a few minutes, he arrived on his scooter.

'Why are you staying in a hotel when you have a friend in the same city? You must move to my home immediately,' he insisted.

I agreed. I had no reason to refuse his warm hospitality.

I shifted to his haveli. Three families lived in the mansion. Each family had a separate kitchen and lived in their own sections of the huge home. Ajay's side of the home had a view of the Ganga with the evening lights shining brightly as far as I could see.

His wife, Nishi, entertained me with delicious Kashi sweets, sumptuous food and paan. Later, he took me to a Hindustani music concert and spoke about the great musicians of Kashi such as Bismillah Khan and Ravi Shankar and how the city was also a place for music lovers. The city, though dirty, was thriving with life and culture.

At dawn, I found myself at the Gai ghat ready for the dip. I sat alone on the steps and then immersed myself in the water till my shoulder blades. The coldness took me by surprise and it took a few minutes for my body to adjust to this new temperature.

I took some water in my palms and my mind instantly went back to Avva. There she was—wearing the green sari and the yellow blouse, looking at me with love and telling me about the three handfuls of water from the Ganga. I saw Kaka sitting on the verandah during sunset, telling me how it was Lord Vishwanath who decided when an individual visited Kashi. How my old grandparents had loved the city and the river Ganga! Tears sprang to my eyes. I was blessed to have grandparents who were content and had such strong beliefs.

'It is so easy to visit Kashi now,' I thought. 'I took a flight from Bengaluru to Delhi and then to Varanasi and reached in a mere five hours.' Now, there was no Kashi Samaradhane or the customary distribution of the holy water or the black thread. Nobody had the time or the inclination.

I looked at the rising sun and was brought back to the present moment. I took the first handful of water and said to myself, 'O Ganga, with the sun as the witness, I give this water on behalf of my grandparents. May their souls rest in peace and be happy wherever they are right now.'

I felt relieved and knew that I had fulfilled my grandparents' desire even though they had never told me to do so.

Then I cupped some more water and said out loud, 'O Ganga, with the sun as the witness, you are the lifeline of our country. You have seen the rise and fall of many kingdoms on your banks. I am grateful and proud to belong to this land.

May you continue to flourish. There is nothing that I can give you but this handful of water.'

With the third handful, I remembered my grandfather's words, 'Give up what you love the most.'

'What should I detach myself from?' I wondered. I loved life, colours, shapes, nature, music, art forms, reading and shopping, especially for saris. My selection of earthy colours was popular and I loved observing the changes in sari designs over the years. 'Well, if the city of Kashi demands what I love the most, then with the sun as the witness, I give up all kinds of shopping from this day on, except for essentials like food, medicine, travel, books and music. I will do so until the day I am no longer in this world,' I said and completed the ritual.

Slowly, I released the water from my palms back to the Ganga.

Somewhere out there, it felt like my grandfather had just smiled. A few minutes later, I waded out of the water and sat on the steps with a towel wrapped around me.

So there would be no more appreciation of my sari choices and none of my friends would call me for wedding shopping. I was worried if I would be able to stick to my vow since I had planned to buy saris that day in Kashi. I wondered if I had chosen to give up shopping on the spur of the moment or if it was pre-planned somehow. To this day, I don't know.

I got up, changed my clothes, took out the kumkum powder from Avva's bharani and put a bit on my forehead.

That was twenty years ago.

The truth is that the vow turned out to be a gateway to freedom. The desire to acquire has vanished over time. Once a year, a few known friends and sisters gave me saris of their choice and I continued to wear them happily for a long time but as the years flew by, I lost interest in that too, and requested them not to gift me anything.

That last handful of water had changed my life forever.

5

Cattle Class

Last year, I was at the Heathrow International Airport in London about to board a flight. Usually, I wear a sari even when I am abroad, but I prefer wearing a salwar kameez while travelling. So there I was—a senior citizen dressed in typical Indian apparel at the terminal gate.

Since the boarding hadn't started, I sat down and began to observe my surroundings. The flight was bound for Bengaluru and so I could hear people around me chatting in Kannada. I saw many old married couples of my age—they were most likely coming back from the US or UK after helping their children either through childbirth or a new home. I saw some British business executives talking to each other about India's progress. Some teenagers were busy with the gadgets in their hands while the younger children were crying or running about the gate.

After a few minutes, the boarding announcement was made and I joined the queue. The woman in front of me was a well-groomed lady in an Indo-Western silk outfit, a Gucci handbag and high heels. Every single strand of her hair was in place and a friend stood next to her in an expensive silk sari, pearl necklace, matching earrings and delicate diamond bangles.

I looked at the vending machine nearby and wondered if I should leave the queue to get some water.

Suddenly, the woman in front of me turned sideways and looked at me with what seemed like pity in her eyes. Extending her hand, she asked, 'May I see your boarding pass, please?'

I was about to hand over my pass to her, but since she didn't seem like an airline employee, I asked, 'Why?'

'Well, this line is meant for business class travellers only,' she said confidently and pointed her finger towards the economy class queue. 'You should go and stand there,' she said.

I was about to tell her that I had a business class ticket but on second thoughts, held back. I wanted to know why she had thought that I wasn't worthy of being in the business class. So I repeated, 'Why should I stand there?'

She sighed. 'Let me explain. There is a big difference in the price of an economy and a business class ticket. The latter costs almost two and a half times more than . . .'

'I think it is three times more,' her friend interrupted.

'Exactly,' said the woman. 'So there are certain privileges that are associated with a business class ticket.'

'Really?' I decided to be mischievous and pretended not to know. 'What kind of privileges are you talking about?'

She seemed annoyed. 'We are allowed to bring two bags but you can only take one. We can board the flight from another, less-crowded queue. We are given better meals and seats. We can extend the seats and lie down flat on them. We always have television screens and there are four washrooms for a small number of passengers.'

Her friend added, 'A priority check-in facility is available for our bags, which means they will come first upon arrival and we get more frequent flyer miles for the same flight.'

'Now that you know the difference, you can go to the economy line,' insisted the woman.

'But I don't want to go there.' I was firm.

The lady turned to her friend. 'It is hard to argue with these cattle-class people. Let the staff come and instruct her where to go. She isn't going to listen to us.'

I didn't get angry. The word 'cattle class' was like a blast from the past and reminded me of another incident.

One day, I had gone to an upscale dinner party in my home city of Bengaluru. Plenty of local celebrities and socialites were in attendance. I was speaking to some guests in Kannada, when a man came to me and said very slowly and clearly in English, 'May I introduce myself? I am . . .'

It was obvious that he thought that I might have a problem understanding the language.

I smiled. 'You can speak to me in English.'

'Oh,' he said, slightly flabbergasted. 'I'm sorry. I thought you weren't comfortable with English because I heard you speaking in Kannada.'

'There's nothing shameful in knowing one's native language. It is, in fact, my right and my privilege. I only speak in English when somebody can't understand Kannada.'

The line in front of me at the airport began moving forward and I came out of my reverie. The two women ahead were whispering among themselves, 'Now she will be sent to the other line. It is so long now! We tried to tell her but she refused to listen to us.'

When it was my turn to show my boarding pass to the attendant, I saw them stop and wait a short distance away, waiting to see what would happen. The attendant took my boarding pass and said brightly, 'Welcome back! We met last week, didn't we?'

'Yes,' I replied.

She smiled and moved on to the next traveller.

I walked a few steps ahead of the women intending to let this go, but then I changed my mind and came back. 'Please tell me—what made you think that I couldn't afford a business class ticket? Even if I didn't have one, was it really your prerogative to tell me where I should stand? Did I ask you for help?'

The women stared at me in silence.

'You refer to the term "cattle class". Class does not mean possession of a huge amount of money,' I continued, unable to stop myself from giving them a piece of my mind. 'There are plenty of wrong ways to earn money in this world. You may be rich enough to buy comfort and luxuries, but the same money doesn't define class or give you the ability to purchase it. Mother Teresa was a classy woman. So is Manjul Bhargava, a great mathematician of Indian origin. The concept that you automatically gain class by acquiring money is an outdated thought process.'

I left without waiting for a reply.

Approximately eight hours later, I reached my destination. It was a weekday and I rushed to office as soon as I could only to learn that my day was going to be spent in multiple meetings. A few hours later, I requested my program director to handle the last meeting of the day by herself as I was already starting to feel tired and jet lagged.

'I am really sorry, but your presence is essential for that discussion,' she replied. 'Our meeting is with the organization's CEO and she is keen to meet you in person. She has been following up with me for a few months now and though I have communicated our decision, she feels that a discussion with you will change the outcome. I have already informed her that the decision will not be reversed irrespective of whom she meets, but she refuses to take me at my word. I urge you to meet her and close this chapter.'

I wasn't new to this situation and reluctantly agreed.

Time went by quickly and soon, I had to go in for the last meeting of the day. Just then, I received an emergency call.

'Go ahead with the meeting,' I said to the program director. 'I will join you later.'

When I entered the conference room after fifteen minutes, I saw the same women from the airport in the middle of a presentation. To my surprise, they were simply dressed—one was wearing a simple khadi sari while the other wore an unglamorous salwar kameez. The clothes were a reminder of the stereotype that is still rampant today. Just like one is expected to wear the finest of silks for a wedding, social workers must present themselves in a plain and uninteresting manner. When they saw me, there was an awkward pause that lasted for only a few seconds before one of them acknowledged my presence and continued the presentation as if nothing had happened.

'My coffee estate is in this village. All the estate workers' children go to a government school nearby. Many are sharp and intelligent but the school has no facilities. The building doesn't even have a roof or clean drinking water. There are no benches, toilets or library. You can see children in the school . . .'

'But no teachers,' I completed the sentence.

She nodded and smiled. 'We request the foundation to be generous and provide the school with proper facilities, including an auditorium, so that the poor kids can enjoy the essentials of a big school.'

My program director opened her mouth to say something, but I signalled her to stop.

'How many children are there in the school?' I asked.

'Around 250.'

'How many of them are the children of the estate workers?'

'All of them. My father got the school sanctioned when he was the MLA,' she said proudly.

'Our foundation helps those who don't have any godfathers or godmothers. Think of the homeless man on the road or the daily-wage worker. Most of them have no one they can run to in times of crisis. We help the children of such people. The estate workers help your business prosper and in return, you can afford to help them. In fact, it is your duty to do so. Helping them also helps you in the long run, but it is the foundation's internal policy to work for the disadvantaged in projects where all the benefits go directly and solely to the underprivileged alone. Maybe this concept is beyond the understanding of the cattle class.'

Both the women looked at each other, unsure of how to respond.

I looked at my program director and said, 'Hey, I want to tell you a story.'

I could see from her face that she was feeling awkward. A story in the middle of a serious meeting?

I began, 'George Bernard Shaw was a great thinker of his times. One day, a dinner was arranged at a British club in his honour. The rules of the club mandated that the men wear a suit and a tie. It was probably the definition of class in those days.

'Bernard Shaw, being who he was, walked into the club in his usual casual attire. The doorman looked at him and said very politely, "Sorry, sir, I cannot allow you to enter the premises."

'"Why not?"

'"You aren't following the dress code of the club, sir."

'"Well, today's dinner is in my honour, so it is my words that matter, not what I wear," replied Bernard, perfectly reasonable in his explanation.

'"Sir, whatever it may be, I can't allow you inside in these clothes."

'Shaw tried to convince the doorman but he wouldn't budge from his stance. So he walked all the way back to his house, changed into appropriate clothes and entered the club.

'A short while later, the room was full, with people sitting in anticipation of his speech. He stood up to address the audience, but first removed his coat and tie and placed it on a chair. "I am not going to talk today," he announced.

'There were surprised murmurs in the audience. Those who knew him personally asked him about the reason for his out-of-character behaviour.

'Shaw narrated the incident that happened a while ago and said, "When I wore a coat and tie, I was allowed to come inside. My mind is in no way affected by the clothes I wear. This means that to all of you who patronize the club, the clothes are more important than my brain. So let the coat and the tie take my place instead."

'Saying thus, he walked out of the room.'

I stood up. 'The meeting is over,' I said. We exchanged cursory goodbyes and I walked back to my room.

My program director followed me, 'Your decision regarding the school was right. But what was that other story all about? And why now? What is this cattle-class business? I didn't understand a thing!'

I smiled at her obvious confusion. 'Only the cattle-class folks will understand what happened back there. You don't worry about it.'

6

A Life Unwritten

It was the year 1943. My father was a young medical doctor posted in a small dispensary in a village known as Chandagad, located on the border of the two states of Maharashtra and Karnataka. It rained continuously for eight months there and the only activity during the remaining four months was tree cutting. It was a lesser-known and thinly populated village surrounded by a thick and enormous forest. Since British officers came to hunt in the jungle, a small clinic was set up there for their convenience. None of the villagers went there because they preferred using the local medicines and plants. So there was nobody in the clinic except my father.

Within a week of his transfer there, my father started getting bored. He was uprooted from the lively city of Pune to this slow and silent village where there seemed to be no people at all! He had no contact with the outside world—his only companion was the calendar on the wall. Sometimes, he would go for a walk outside but when he heard the roar of the tigers in the jungle nearby, he would get scared and walk back to the clinic as fast as he could. It was no wonder then that he was too afraid to step out at night because of the snakes that were often seen slithering on the ground.

One winter morning, he heard heavy breathing outside his main door and bravely decided to peep through the window. He saw a tigress stretching and yawning in the verandah with her cubs by her side. Paralysed with fear, my father did not open the door the entire day. On another day, he opened the window only to find snakes hanging from the roof in front of his house—almost like ropes.

My father wondered if he was transferred to the village as a form of punishment for something he may have done. But there was nothing that he could do to change the situation.

One night, he finished an early dinner and began reading a book in the light of a kerosene lamp. It was raining heavily outside.

Suddenly, he heard a knock on the door. 'Who could it be?' he wondered.

When he opened it, he saw four men wrapped in woollen rugs with sticks in their hands. They said to him in Marathi, 'Doctor Sahib, take your bag and come with us immediately.'

My father barely understood their rustic Marathi. He protested. 'But the clinic is closed and look at the time!'

The men were in no mood to listen—they pushed him and loudly demanded that he accompany them. Quietly, my father picked up his bag and followed them like a lamb to the bullock cart waiting for them. The pouring rain and the moonless night disoriented him and while he didn't know where they were taking him, he sensed that the drive might take some time.

Using all the courage he had left, he asked, 'Where are you taking me?'

There was no reply.

It was a few hours before they reached their destination and the bullock cart came to a complete halt. In the light of a kerosene lamp, somebody escorted them. My father noticed the paddy fields around him and in the middle of it all, he saw a house. The minute he set foot in the house, a female voice said, 'Come, come. The patient is here in this room.'

For the first time since he had come to the village, my father felt that he could finally put his medical expertise to good use. The patient was a young girl, approximately sixteen years old. An old lady was standing near the girl who was obviously in labour. My father turned pale. He went back to the other room and told her family, 'Look, I haven't been trained in delivering a baby and I am a male doctor. You must call someone else.'

But the family refused to listen. 'That's not an option. You must do what needs to be done and we will pay you handsomely,' they insisted. 'The baby may be delivered alive or dead but the girl must be saved.'

My father pleaded with them. 'Please, I am not interested in the money. Let me go now.'

The men came close, shoved him inside the patient's room and locked the door from outside. My father became afraid. He knew he had no choice. He had observed and assisted in a few deliveries under the guidance of his medical college professors, but nothing more. Nervously, he started recalling his limited past experience and theoretical knowledge as his medical instincts kicked in.

There was no table in the room. So he signalled the old lady, who appeared to be deaf and dumb, to help him set up a makeshift table with the sacks of paddy grains around them. Then my father extracted a rubber sheet from his bag and laid it out neatly on top of the sacks.

He asked the girl to lie down on it and instructed the old lady to boil water and sterilize his instruments. By then, the contraction had passed. The girl was sweating profusely and the doctor even more. She looked at him with big innocent, teary eyes and slowly began, 'Don't save me. I don't want to make it through the night.'

'Who are you?'

'I am the daughter of a big zamindar here,' she said in a soft voice. The rain outside made it hard for him to hear her. 'Since there was no high school in our village, my parents let me study in a distant town. There, I fell in love with one of my classmates. At first, I didn't know that I was pregnant, but once I found out, I told the baby's father who immediately ran away. By the time my parents learnt of what had happened, it was too late to do anything. That's why they sent me here to this godforsaken place where nobody would find out.'

She stopped as a strong contraction hit her.

After a few minutes, she said, 'Doctor, I am sure that once the baby is born, my family will kill the child and beat me violently.' Then she grabbed my father's arms as more tears gathered in her eyes, 'Please don't try to save the baby or me. Just leave me alone here and let me die. That's all I want.'

At first, my father didn't know how to respond. Then he said to her as gently as he could, 'I am a doctor and I can't let a patient die when I know that I can do something to save him or her. You mustn't discourage me from doing my duty.'

The girl fell silent.

The labour was hard, scary and long and finally, my father managed to deliver the baby successfully with the assistance of the old lady. The young girl was exhausted and sweaty at the end of the ordeal. She closed her eyes in despair and didn't even ask to see the baby. Hesitantly, she asked, 'Is it a boy or a girl?'

'It's a girl,' replied my father, while trying to check the baby's vitals.

'Oh my God! It's a girl!' she cried. 'Her life will be just like mine—under the cruel pressure of the men in the family. And she doesn't even have a father!' She began sobbing loudly.

But my father was busy with the baby and barely heard her.

Suddenly, the girl realized that something was wrong, 'Doctor, why isn't the baby crying?' When she didn't get a reply, she continued, 'I will be happy if she doesn't survive. She will be spared from a cursed life.'

My father held the baby upside down, gently slapped her and instantly, the baby's strong cries filled the room. When the men outside heard the baby cry, they opened the door and instructed him, 'Doctor, get ready to leave. We will drop you back.'

My father cleaned up his patient, gathered his instruments and packed his bag. The old lady began cleaning the room. He looked at the troubled young girl and said, 'Take the baby and run away from this place if you can find it in your heart to do so. Go to Pune and look for Pune Nursing School. Find a clerk there called Gokhale and tell him that RH has sent you. He will help you get admission in a nursing course. In time, you will become a nurse and lead an independent life, with the ability to take care of your own needs. Raise your daughter with pride. Don't you dare leave her behind or else she will end up suffering like you. That's my most sincere advice for you.'

'But, doctor, how will I go to Pune? I don't even know where it is!'

'Go to the nearest city of Belgaum and then from there, you can take a bus to Pune.'

My father said goodbye to her and came out of the room.

An old man handed him one hundred rupees. 'Doctor, these are your fees for helping the girl with the delivery. I warn you—don't say a word about what happened here today. If you do, I will learn of it and your head will no longer be attached to the rest of your body.'

My father nodded, suddenly overtaken by a sense of calm. 'I'm sorry,' he said. 'I think I forgot my scissors in the room. I will need it tomorrow at the clinic.'

He turned around and went back inside and saw the young girl gazing at the sleeping newborn with tears in her eyes. When the old lady's back was turned towards him, my father handed over the money to the girl. 'This is all I have with me right now,' he said. 'Use it and do what I have told you.'

'Doctor, what is your name?' she asked.

'My name is Dr R.H. Kulkarni, but almost everyone calls me RH. Be brave, child. Goodbye and good luck.'

My father left the room and the house. The return journey was equally rough and he finally reached home at dawn. He was dead tired and soon, sleep took over. The next morning, his mind wandered back to his first patient in the village and his first earning. He became aware of his shortcomings and wished he was better qualified in gynaecology. However, his current shortage of funds made him postpone the dream for another day.

A few months later, he got married and shared his dream of becoming a gynaecologist with his wife.

Time passed quickly. He was transferred to different places in Maharashtra and Karnataka and had four children along the way. By the time he turned forty-two, the couple had carefully saved enough money for further education and my father decided to pursue his desire. So he left his family in Hubli and joined Egmore Medical College in Chennai, and fulfilled his dream of becoming a gynaecologist surgeon. He was one of the few rare male gynaecologists at the time.

He went back to Hubli and started working in Karnataka Medical College as a professor. His sympathetic manner towards the underprivileged and his genuine concern for the women and girls he treated made him quite popular—both as a doctor and as a teacher. The same concern reflected in his liberal attitude towards his daughters and he allowed them to pursue their chosen fields of education, which was unheard of in those days.

My father was an atheist. 'God doesn't reside in a church, mosque or temple,' he would often say. 'I see him in all my patients. If a woman dies during childbirth, then it is the loss of one patient for a doctor but for that child, it is the lifelong loss of a mother. And tell me, who can replace a mother?'

Despite his retirement, my father's love for learning did not diminish and he remained active.

One day, he went for a medical conference to another city. There, he met a young woman in her thirties. She was presenting cases from her experience in the rural areas. My father found her work interesting and went to tell her so after the presentation. 'Doctor, your research is excellent. I am quite impressed by your work,' he said.

'Thank you,' she said.

Just then, someone called out to my father, 'RH, we are waiting for you to grab some lunch. Will you take long?'

The young woman asked, 'What is your name, doctor?'

'Dr R.H. Kulkarni, or RH.'

After a moment of silence, she asked, 'Were you in Chandagad in 1943?'

'Yes.'

'Doctor, I live in a village around forty kilometres away from here. May I request you to come home right now for a brief visit?'

My father was unprepared for such an invitation. Why was she calling him to her house?

'Maybe some other time, doctor,' he replied, hoping to end the matter.

But the woman was persistent, 'You must come. Please. Think of this as a request from someone who has been waiting for you for years now.'

My father was puzzled by her enigmatic answer and still refused, but she pleaded with him. There was something in her eyes—something so desperate—that in the end, he gave in and accompanied her to the village.

On the way to the village, both of them exchanged ideas and she spoke animatedly about her work and her findings. As the two of them approached her residence, my father realized that the house was also a nursing home. He walked in through the front door and saw a lady in her fifties standing in the living room.

The young woman next to him said, 'Ma, this is Dr RH. Is he the one you have been waiting for all these years?'

The woman came forward, bent down and touched her forehead to my father's feet. He felt his feet getting wet from her tears. It was strange. Who were these women? My father didn't know what to do. He quickly bent forward, placed his hands on the older woman's shoulders and pulled her up.

'Doctor, you may not remember me but I can never forget you. Mine must have been your first delivery.'

Still, my father couldn't recognize her.

'A long time ago, you lived in a village on the border of Maharashtra and Karnataka. One night, there was a heavy downpour and you helped me—a young, unmarried girl then—through childbirth. There was no delivery table in the room, so you converted stacks of paddy sacks into a makeshift table. Many hours later, I gave birth to a daughter.'

In a flash, the memories came flooding back and my father recollected that night. 'Of course I remember you!' he said. 'It was the middle of the night and I urged you to go to Pune with your newborn. I think I was as scared as you!'

'You gave me a hundred rupees, which is what my family paid you for the delivery. It was a big amount in those days and still, you handed it all over to me.'

'Yes, my monthly salary was seventy-five rupees then!' added my father with a smile.

'You told me your last name but I couldn't hear it because of the deafening sound of the rain. I took your advice, went to Pune, found your friend Gokhale and became a nurse. It was very, very hard, but I was able to raise my daughter on my own. After such a terrible experience, I wanted my daughter to become a gynaecologist. Luckily, she shared my dream too. Today, she is a doctor and is also married to one and they practise here. At one point, I spent months searching for you but with no luck. Then we heard that you had moved to Karnataka after the reorganization of the state departments in 1956. Meanwhile, Gokhale also passed away and I lost all hope of ever finding you. I prayed to God to give me a chance to meet you and thank you for showing me the right path at the right time.'

My father felt like he was in a Bollywood movie and was enchanted by the unexplained mystery of life. A few kind words and encouragement had changed a young girl's life.

She clasped her hands together, 'We are so grateful to you, doctor. My daughter wanted to call you for the inauguration of the nursing home here and we were very disappointed at not being able to reach you then. Time has passed and now the nursing home is doing very well.'

My father wiped his moist eyes and looked around to see the name of the nursing home. He looked to the right and found himself staring at it—R.H. Diagnostic.

7

No Place Like Home

Infosys Foundation is involved in various types of construction projects like building dharamshalas for poor patients and their caretakers, schools for children in remote areas, houses for the thousands who suffer in calamities such as cyclones and floods, and toilets for both schools and public use in an effort to encourage cleanliness in our country.

From its inception, I wanted the foundation to be independent and have its own office, but during the initial period, we didn't have more than Rs 5000 left in the bank at the end of every financial year, despite the annual funding. Somehow, the will to help others made having our own premises an extremely low priority. Still, the foundation kept short-term fixed deposits and we carefully managed our cash flows to ensure interest, and over the years, we managed to accumulate a sizeable amount.

One day, I learnt of a beautiful plot of land with an old building available for sale in the popular suburb of Jayanagar in Bengaluru. The interest we had saved was just enough to purchase the land. Since the building was not suited for the needs of an office, it was obvious that at some point, we would have to demolish it and build our own. So we decided to leave the land as is until we had saved some more.

The next financial year too, we had less than Rs 5000 in our bank account. Even though we had saved a little interest over the years, the construction cost was higher than the money we had and building our office remained a dream.

Years passed by and finally, in 2002, the foundation was able to accumulate enough interest to begin construction. I was happy. My dream was about to come true. I got the ball rolling, contacted an architect and instructed him to create a simple plan for us.

A few days later, I received an invitation from a Middle Eastern country to speak at a ladies' association there. I decided to accept it because I had some talks scheduled in Dubai and Kuwait soon after. I wanted to complete all my assignments there during one trip and thus save money on the cost of air tickets.

Soon, I was on my way. Like all trips, this one, too, had many meetings and talks lined up. There were also events wherein the who's who of the Indian community in the region was expected to participate. It took courage for most of the people I met to leave their homes behind in India, settle in a foreign country and still hold on to the culture and faith, against many odds. People also spoke about the work we did, or thought we did—sometimes it was factual and sometimes a little exaggerated.

Finally, the day came for my last speaking engagement. It was a good event with lively questions and discussions. When the function drew to a close, I prepared to leave for my hotel.

A few women met me on their way out. 'Ma'am, would you like to buy anything here?' they inquired politely. 'The shopping experience here is quite wonderful. Maybe you'd like some pearls or gold?'

'No,' I replied. 'But is there anything interesting that I can see?'

The women pondered for a moment, shook their heads and said their goodbyes.

Just then, I noticed two women approaching me. One of them said in a low voice, 'Ma'am, we would like to invite you to our small shelter. Will you please consider it?'

'What's there in your shelter?' I asked.

'We want you to see it for yourself. We can tell you about the work we do in various ways, but I don't know which aspect of our work will strike a chord with you.'

My antenna went up. There was something about them and their humble manner that made me curious. I nodded. 'Please give me a few minutes. I will come with you right now,' I said.

I thanked my hosts quickly and left the venue with the women in tow. A short while later, we reached a small house in a residential area. At first glance, it seemed more of an outhouse to me. When we entered, I saw five women there—all in their nightwear. Some of them had swollen eyes and red marks on their cheeks. It was obvious that they were not in the best of health or happy in any way.

Within a few minutes, we were all seated.

'What language should I speak in?' I asked the women who had brought me there.

'Hindi is okay. A little English is also fine.'

The women began telling me their names and the states they were from—one was from Tamil Nadu, two from Andhra Pradesh and one from Kerala.

I exchanged a few pleasantries with them and soon enough, Nazneem, the woman from Andhra Pradesh, started narrating her story, 'Madam, I was a maid in the district of Karimnagar years ago and had three daughters old enough to get married. An agent told me that I would earn much more in the Middle East for the same work I did in India. He told me that I would even get a fifteen-day vacation once a year with free air travel to see my family. I realized that if I worked here for three years, I would save enough to bear the wedding expenses of all my daughters. It was everything I could ask for. Our financial troubles would go away! My husband, who is a vegetable vendor, kept reassuring me that he would look after the girls during my absence. He encouraged me to go as long as I kept in touch regularly. So with my limited savings and by selling all the gold that I had, I paid for my passport, visa, travel fare and the agent's commission.'

Her eyes clouded over as the memories came flooding back. 'When the time came to say goodbye, my heart left heavy and I was afraid. I had never even travelled from Karimnagar to the big city of Hyderabad. Then how would I travel abroad and manage things all alone in a country completely foreign to me? How would I be able to live away from my family?

'The agent assured me, "The family you are going to work for are kind. They are also of the same religion as you. You won't take too much time to adjust. I have already spoken to them. They will treat you as a family member. If you are unhappy, you can come back after a year and not return."

'I felt somewhat relieved and for the first time in my life, I travelled to Hyderabad on my own and then took a flight from the city to come here.'

I interrupted her, 'Were you scared during the flight?'

Nazneem thought for a moment. 'Not really,' she replied. 'In the airplane, I met many women just like me, both young and old, and I felt better knowing that I wasn't alone. Outside the destination airport, we were handed a burka each and were directed to a bus. The heat was unbearable, and it felt like I was almost on fire. Karimnagar is a hot place in India but the level of heat in this country cannot be described. Despite the scorching heat, the bus was not air-conditioned. We were all expecting a luxurious bus, like the one the agent had promised. We dismissed it as an error or a problem with bus availability. In fact, most of us believed that it might rain soon—like it happens in some parts of south India.

'An hour-long ride later, the bus dropped us at a location from where we were taken to different houses for our new jobs.

'The house I was taken to was huge, beautiful and air-conditioned. I was given a tiny room near the kitchen. First, I met the house manager who took my passport and handed me some cleaning supplies and told me something in a language I didn't understand. Thankfully, there was another woman housekeeper from India named Santosh who translated everything for me: "Your work begins right now. Start cleaning the whole house and make it spotless. Madam has no tolerance for dust. Your meal timings are— breakfast at 9 a.m., lunch at 3 p.m. and dinner at 10 p.m. Also, you must wear a burka whenever you go outside the house."

'I took some time to unpack my bags and use the bathroom. Then I went back to search for Santosh. The supplies were good and Santosh taught me how to use them and introduced me to some of the electronic cleaning equipment too.

'Over the next few days, I hardly saw the owner of the house—she was either out of the country or living on a different floor. I always reported to the house manager.

'Santosh and I began to get to know one another. One afternoon, when we had a few minutes alone, she asked me, "Why did you come here? This isn't such a good work environment. We work like donkeys from morning to night with minimal rest and sometimes, we have to endure the wrath of the house manager for no fault of ours. Though we have come for household chores, we always get burdened with extra work. Look at me—I help in the kitchen, bathe all the young children, iron all the clothes and wash all the dishes. Now, they have brought you here to clean the house, but that's not the only work you will be assigned. You may have to do the cook's job when he doesn't show up or run errands as and when needed."

'"It doesn't matter as long as I get a good salary," I replied honestly.

'"That's what I used to think too," said Santosh. There was sadness in her eyes. "We don't get a rupee in our hands. Sometimes, the owner says that the money has been deposited in a bank account or that it has been sent to our family. It's been a year since I came here but I haven't received any payment directly."

'"But our agent said . . ."

'"It doesn't matter what your agent said or who he is— they are all the same. They have lied to us and lured us into this country and job. We are poor and we fell for the hope they gave us. They know that once we get here, it is difficult to return. The agents know that we are all alone here. In this country, we can't even go out without a man accompanying us. The owners also keep our passports with them, making it impossible to leave this place."

'For the first time since landing there, I became afraid. I didn't know what to do. "Santosh, you have been here for a year. When are you going back? Are you going to quit work or change jobs?"

'"We can't quit or change jobs without the owner's consent. Most of the bosses don't allow it. So I am trying my best to return, but I need money for a one-way ticket and my passport."

'"Do you talk to your family back home?"

'"Yes, I write letters and hand them over to my agent, but I don't know whether it reaches them. I haven't received even one reply yet. I only get to hear what the agent tells me about my family. I know that they have tried to call me here on the phone, but there are strict instructions against that according to the rules of this house. Madam doesn't want her staff to take personal calls on her landlines.

Moreover, I know that it isn't easy for them to call me here, and I don't want to share my difficulties with them. I hear that a lump sum amount is sent to them every six months. But once I get my ticket, I will go back and never come back here."

'I was slightly relieved to hear that her family was getting some money. "Aren't they supposed to send the money every month?" I asked.

'"The agents are much smarter than us. They keep a salary backlog of at least six months. If I go back to my country and don't return, then they will keep that money. So many people come back for their money and the cycle continues. To someone in our financial position, a six-month salary is a big amount to walk away from."

'"When are you planning to go home?"

'"It depends on the owners. Sometimes, they send the workers home after fifteen months or sometimes after two years. I don't know when they will decide to send me back. I can understand their language now but still pretend not to. I have learnt that Madam is going to India to enjoy the monsoon in Kerala. Since I am from the state and know the local language, she wants me to go with her and look after the children. I will ask her then to allow me to visit my family for a few days and if she does, I won't come back. I have reached a point where I don't even care about the money," said Santosh firmly.

'I could not sleep that night. Had I been duped by the agent? How much money will my family really get? With not many options at my disposal, I decided that the best way forward was to keep a low profile and continue working.

'For the first few weeks, things seemed okay. The staff was usually given leftover food, which was good and I didn't have any complaints related to work. After some time had passed, I started getting extra chores, especially around the time Madam was leaving for a vacation to India. Santosh was going to go with them too and I knew that she wouldn't come back. So I wrote letters to my family and requested her to mail them from India.

'Once Santosh and the family left the country, the house manager instructed me to take on all of Santosh's work as well. Since the owner always entertained guests in his big mansion, there was a lot of cooking and cleaning to be done. There were a total of fourteen children in the house and each child would also frequently bring his or her friends over. I felt trapped—like a bird in a cage. Since the work more than doubled, my efficiency reduced and the house manager became upset and refused to listen to my concerns. She would show me a stick and say, "Don't complain about your work. You are being paid for it. I don't want to hear another word."

'When the unending workload became unbearable during the day, I would sit down and rest for a few minutes. If the house manager found me resting, she would beat me with that same stick. That's when I recalled the marks on Santosh's hand and realized how she had got them. Nobody ever beat me in my home. Though we were poor, we lived with dignity.

'The loneliness and the excess work soon began affecting my health and my ability to work. I longed for my family, my children and my friends. As the days went by, there was nothing but sadness left in my soul.'

I interjected, 'With whom did you share your troubles with, now that Santosh was gone?'

'Nobody,' said Nazneem. 'There was a male gardener who would visit and tend to the lawn and plants outside the house, but I could not speak to him according to the country's rules. I couldn't go out as I only had three nightdresses that I wore day and night. I was not allowed to wear the clothes that I had brought with me. I was only allowed to go shopping with the family, and even then, I had to wear a burka on top of my clothes. So I had no friends or acquaintances to speak to.

'Soon, Madam came back from India, upset and furious. She said to the house manager, "Start keeping a close eye on these Indian women. Santosh never came back after she went home. She cheated me. So for now, don't allow this woman to go home any time soon."

'These words dampened my spirit and I cried in the shadows, wondering when I would see my family again.

'One morning, I overheard a conversation between Madam and the house manager. "Whatever you say, Indian women are the best for household work," she told the manager. "They do their jobs quietly, don't answer back or complain too much."

'The house manager said something unintelligible.

'"Recruit two more," she instructed.

'While I hated the thought of somebody else going through what I had endured, I was at the end of my rope and hoped that this would reduce my workload in the course of time.

'Weeks later, I was down with high fever.'

'Did you go the doctor?' I couldn't contain myself.

'No, the house manager gave me Crocin. We were never taken to the doctor for any reason whatsoever. I had to work despite the fever. A day later, it went up further and I was afraid that my body would give up. Desperate, I approached the manager and asked her to take me to the nearest doctor or hospital.

'She was blunt, "We have multiple house guests today and I really don't have the time."

'I almost broke down. "I can't work today," I said tearfully. "I am in pain and there's a constant throbbing in my head."

'Nonchalantly, she heated up a spoon on the kitchen fire, caught my hand and pressed the hot spoon on my wrist.

'I screamed and she shushed me. "Don't scream. Nobody will come to help you. You are a servant and must behave like one. Go and start working now," she said, her volume matching mine.

'My body started trembling with fear. Was this going to be my fate till I die?

'I don't remember the days ahead with clarity, but the fever came down and my body, at least, felt a little better. But I was dead inside. I had no incentive to wake up in the mornings, but I had no choice. I lived like a robot. When I had time to think, I only thought about returning home to my family.

'One rare day, when there was nobody at home but me, the gardener, Maruti, requested me for a cup of tea. I wore the burka and went to the backyard to give it to him.

'"Please help me get home," I told him as soon as he started sipping the tea. "I don't know anyone here and you know how they treat the helps in this house. My family wouldn't even get to know if something happened to me here. You are like my brother. Please, can you lend me a hand?"

'"Don't even think of running away," he said. I could see that he was afraid. "If the authorities trace you and bring you back, you will suffer unspeakable cruelty. Still, I will try and speak to a few people I know. I will get back to you."

'I touched his feet. It was as if Allah had come to help me through this kind man.

'A month passed before Maruti approached me at a time when we were alone again. It was Eid, a religious holiday, and the family had gone out for the evening. "I met two kind women at an Indian function. I think they may be able to help you," he said.

'"I am so grateful to you. How did you meet them?"

'"The owner once asked me to deliver some flowers to a government official who was attending an Indian wedding ceremony. At the wedding, I was told to wait and that's when I heard about these two women from others. I somehow managed to see them. Since I am a man and free to move about in this country, I was able to meet them a few more times. I told them about your difficulties here. They have told me to inform you that it is risky to leave your work here, but if you decide to do so and go to them, then they will also share the risk with you and try their best to send you back home. I can take you to them. But do it when you go shopping as it will be easier to escape from there."

'I nodded. We decided to wait for the right moment.

'Meanwhile, Maruti gave me a map and the directions to the place I would have to locate when the time came. I memorized everything well so that I could reach there without any confusion. Maruti had already done more than I could have ever imagined and I decided not to involve him further. The punishment for such actions is severe in this country.

'Weeks later, Madam asked me to run an errand. This was my chance.

'I wore a burka, went to the marketplace, bought groceries and handed them to the driver. I told him that I needed to go to the restroom and that I would be back soon. The moment I was out of sight of the driver, I ran! The driver would have taken some time to realize that I was missing. As many women wore the burka, I knew that it would be tough for him to find me. I kept going with my heart beating fast— sometimes I ran and sometimes I walked. Within half an hour, I reached my destination with nothing but the clothes I was wearing. Finally, I was here.'

Nazneem's story ended and she collapsed on the chair, tired from reliving the dark past.

The two women turned to me. 'She came two days ago,' one of them said.

A silence fell in the room. 'No one should have to go through this,' I thought.

Gracy, the woman from Kerala, broke the stillness in the room by sharing her story. She was beautiful and well-spoken. She had also been duped by an agent who had promised her a job to tutor children. And yet, her story was vastly different.

Gracy was an orphan who grew up in a government home for such children. She became a teacher in a convent school and though the salary was enough to get by, it was not enough to achieve her dream of owning a small home. In time, Gracy found a boy she liked but he did not have a steady job or income. Since they didn't have any assets, they made a mutual decision—Gracy would go abroad for tutoring. This would give the couple a chance to earn enough money to purchase a home later and settle down.

When she reached the home she was going to live in, she was quite shocked to find that her employer had four wives and sixteen children—all of whom lived in the huge residence. However, only ten of the boys and girls were old enough to go to pre-school, primary or middle school. Gracy taught the children subjects such as English, mathematics, history, art and craft and manners. For a few years, things seemed all right and she was treated fairly well. She was paid once in six months in bulk and her employer even allowed her a paid vacation to India once a year. The children had also become very fond of her, and she was not mistreated like Nazneem.

As the years passed and the boys reached their mid-teens, their classmates and cousins began frequenting the home. Soon, she became the target of their lecherous stares and she realized for the first time that she was an easy target should they wish to approach her. She became extremely uncomfortable living there. When she tried to share her concerns with one of the employer's wives, she scoffed at her, 'Yes, Gracy, you are so beautiful that many men will desire you. In fact, I won't be surprised if my husband does too!'

From that day on, Gracy became afraid for herself. She began to avoid teaching the older boys and even told the employer that they did not need her help any more, but nobody listened.

'You are paid to teach the children and you must fulfil your responsibility. There's nothing more to say,' said the employer and dismissed her with a wave of his hand.

One day, a friend of the boys came to her room and tried to forcefully kiss her. Due to her presence of mind, she managed to push him out of the room with all her might and didn't mention it to anyone.

The next day, however, she found that one of the boys named Abdul was very upset.

Upon further inquiry, Abdul said, 'My friend is upset for some reason. When I asked him to come home today, he refused and said that it was because of you. Tell me, what have you done?'

Gracy found it hard to share her troubles with a sixteen-year-old, but thought it wise to tell the truth to her ward.

To her astonishment, he laughed. 'You are very attractive,' said Abdul. 'I can't blame my friend for not being able to control himself. If you were ugly like the cook, Fatima, then nobody would want you.'

'Abdul, I am your teacher,' said Gracy very firmly, despite the tremors she was beginning to feel in her body. 'How dare you speak to me like this?'

'I am no longer a child. I am a man now and look at women from a different perspective,' he responded and walked away casually.

'It was then that I realized that the home was a ticking time bomb for me. I was better off living in a rented house in my country than staying under such duress in that residence. Nobody—neither the employer nor his wives—was going to protect me if something were to happen. I was fortunate enough that my passport was with me. And yet, I had no money. But I knew these two kind women here who helped women in such distress.'

'How did you get to know about them?' I asked.

'It was a stroke of luck. Last December, I had attended a Christmas party. It was there that I met them and learnt about their work. Once the time was right, I walked to the shelter, leaving all of my belongings at my employer's home,' she said, staring at the floor.

There was nothing for me to say. I felt ashamed and disgusted at the world today where half of the population does not feel safe.

The two other women—Roja from Tamil Nadu and Neena from Andhra Pradesh—shared their stories with bouts of tears. Their experiences were worse. Each had travelled a different path but both had been raped by their employers.

I couldn't hold back my tears any longer. What a wretched life these women have had! How does one even begin to get over such trauma? It took me a few minutes to compose myself.

I glanced at the two women sitting near me. How did they send these women back?

One of them said, 'Once these women come to the shelter, we go to the Indian embassy and get new passports made for them. It is difficult and at times, we run into problems that cause delays. But the real problem is their departure from here. Legally, we can't keep them in the shelter beyond a certain period of time and we have to buy a one-way ticket for them as soon as we can. And if we have to book it at short notice, we have to almost always pay a high price for it.'

'Who pays for the tickets?'

'We ask around and reach out to everyone we can. The folks in small-paying jobs are high in number but they usually have their own financial problems and other issues. People who do have the money don't really want to support us for a long time. Some would rather buy gold in the souk or hold a party for their friends and families. The rich folks consider this a perennial problem. They are willing to help us for one or two cases but our shelter gets around five women every month. Sooner or later, the donor stops funding the tickets. Sometimes, store owners anonymously buy flight tickets, but everybody is afraid of getting caught some day. Others shrug it off and say that it isn't their problem. They accuse the women of following the path of money. They feel it was their responsibility to verify the agency before coming here. When we began the shelter a few years ago, we pumped in our personal funds. But we aren't rich either and I fear that we won't be able to keep up for long.'

It was a depressing thought. The shelter was a ray of hope for the women caught in difficult circumstances. Where would they go without such a place to run to?

I looked at the clock. It was time to leave for my meeting with a friend. So I said my goodbyes and left the shelter with a heavy heart.

We drove past beautiful homes, wide roads and fancy cars. I felt nothing. All I could think of were the four women and their haunting pasts. Suddenly, I changed my mind.

'Take a U-turn,' I told the driver.

I went back to the shelter and met the two women. I said, 'Infosys Foundation is happy to sponsor one-way tickets for the women in need—be it to their city, village or town. We will take care of the travel cost as long as the shelter has verified them. But you must help them obtain a passport in time and ensure that they are able to board the flight without any hassles.'

The women smiled and agreed.

I smiled back. Finally, I felt like I had lessened some of my burden.

'Tell these women that India is changing,' I told them. 'Gone are the days when people worked for a minuscule salary. In cities, when both the husband and the wife have to go to work, they need a reliable and good housekeeper at home, without which many women choose to quit their jobs. Honesty carries a high price in India now and more and more people are choosing to stay back in the country of their own volition due to the demand in urban areas.'

'The women will be ecstatic to learn of this development,' said one of them. She couldn't stop smiling. 'May God bless the foundation and you for such an invaluable gesture.'

The next day, on my flight back, I couldn't help but think how fortunate we are to live in India. We may not be the richest or the best country in the world, but we have so much freedom. We can switch jobs easily or relocate to a different town or city. If nothing else, most of us have a family that will at least give us a place to stay in times of trouble. We really don't know how lucky we are until we are out of the country.

Out of habit, I began calculating the approximate travel expenses for the women. They had mentioned an average of twenty to twenty-five cases per year. 'This extra annual grant would evaporate my savings for the office building in five years,' I thought, a tad disappointed.

I had to make a choice—build the office or give shelter to these women. I knew, of course, that there really was no choice at all. There was no second-guessing my decision. My conscience and I could still live in a rented three-room space for a few more years.

This happened fifteen years ago.

Last year, we finally moved into our own office and home after twenty years. I named the building 'Neralu'— the shelter.

8

A Powerful Ambassador

I am a storyteller at heart, so it isn't surprising that I fell in love with movies.

When we were children, Bollywood was very different from what it is today. Most movies were in black and white. Then, there were Eastmancolor movies and black and white movies with some songs in colour, until finally, the move was made to colour feature films.

Meena Kumari's tragedies often brought tears to my eyes while Madhubala and Asha Parekh's beautiful song sequences remain etched in my mind. I can't let go of Sadhana and Waheeda Rahman's effortless beauty, while Sanjeev Kumar's powerful acting and Rajesh Khanna's charisma will remain with my generation until we are gone.

I have followed the evolution of Bollywood through the use of technology and also from simple innocent romances to the aggressive and bold portrayal of it today and from classical dances to the drill-team type of dances to breakdance and now, twerking.

Movies were generally taboo in those days and considered a luxury in a village such as mine. We lived in Shiggaon without access to a movie theatre. Besides, there was no electricity in those days. But to our absolute delight, we did get touring talkies in the summer, which were tents set up specifically to screen movies. It was the Lord's answer to our desperation! If we really wanted to see a film, we were accompanied by an adult and our chaperone would decide which movie we would watch. We could only see religious and inspiring movies such as *Sri Krishna Tulabharam*, *Rama Vanavasa* and *Girija Kalyana*. Occasionally, an exception was made and we were allowed to watch a children's movie under adult supervision. We would then go and tell our friends about it. On the big day, my cousins and I would eat early and fill our stomachs so that we wouldn't have to take a break during the movie. We would talk about the film for days on end after the screening. However, the movie-watching days were rare throughout the year.

But nothing stays the same forever. Life changed and I came to the small city of Hubli for my education where there were plenty of movie theatres. And yet, the taboo remained—a teenage girl shouldn't see romantic scenes. So while I happily saw them when I went with my friends, I had to listen to my aunt and close my eyes when I saw the same scenes with her or other senior members of the family.

As the months went past, I became bolder. At the end of every exam season, a bunch of us girls would go together to the movies. We would lie to our families that we were going for a film like *Dashavathara* (about the ten avatars of Lord

Vishnu) and go watch a film of the dreamy hero Rajendra Kumar. All of us had secret crushes on the heroes but we felt awkward sharing this with each other.

When I made it to college, I became what must have been considered 'really bold'. I told my parents, 'I refuse to watch religious films. I have seen enough of them to last me a lifetime. Now, I want to see Rajesh Khanna's movies.'

I lived in a joint family and it was clear that the elders in the family felt astonished and perhaps a little embarrassed at my intensely transparent desire to watch a superstar's movies, especially a hero known for his ridiculous good looks and charm and the ability to drive away all common sense from a girl's mind.

From that day on, my aunt kept a close watch on my grades. The slightest hint of a fall would earn me the comment, 'It is no wonder that your marks are going down. The crappy romantic movies have distracted you and you are no longer able to focus as much as you should.'

Poor Rajesh Khanna was often blamed for my cousins' and my low marks. If only he had known!

Later, I made my way to Bengaluru for my post-graduation. It was heaven! The area known as Majestic boasted of at least thirty movie theatres such as Sangam, Alankar, Kempe Gowda and Majestic, on either side of the road. I frequently managed to watch two movies in one trip.

Once I was left to my own devices in the working ladies' hostel in Pune, there was absolutely no one to stop me and my love for films grew by leaps and bounds. It grew to such an extent that I could study only when movie soundtracks were playing in the background. Many of the students made fun of me.

One day, a few girls gathered at a friend's home.

Someone said to me, 'Movies are a wonderful source of entertainment. But it is like eating dessert every day. It is not good for your health and you will start disliking it at some point.'

'No way,' I protested. 'You can eat different desserts on different days and you'll never reach a point of disliking it. It's the same thing with movies.'

'Easy to say. Not so easy to implement. Are you willing to see a movie every day?'

'Of course I am.' I had no doubt that I could.

My friends were quite thrilled. 'Well, then let's bet on it. If you see 365 movies in 365 days, we will give you one hundred rupees and honour you as Miss Cinema.'

I nodded, quite excited. Thus I began my filmi journey.

Pune was a great city for watching movies. In those days, Nilayam Theatre would screen Raj Kapoor movies—a different one each day. There, I saw all his movies—from the earliest one to the most recent. Once that was done, I switched to the famous director–actor Guru Dutt and watched all his movies in Lakshmi Narayan Theatre. Boredom was nowhere in sight. Just when that was nearing its end, Prabhat Film Company, a pioneer in Marathi movies, began showing their films in Natraj Theatre, which was a stone's throw from my hostel. Some of these were movies from before my time and were those my father had seen when he was a student. So I watched them too—*Manoos*, *Kunku*, *Shejari* and *Ramshastri*, among others. During the days movies were in short supply, I stocked up on English classics at Rahul 70 mm Theatre— *Gone with the Wind, To Sir with Love, Come September, The Ten Commandments*, films featuring Charlie Chaplin, Laurel and Hardy, and other silent movies with subtitles. Occasionally, Deccan Theatre screened Kannada movies too.

At the end of the year, I had successfully watched 365 movies and became such an expert that I could rate any movie that my friends could think of. I even understood the fundamentals for a movie's successful run. Necessary prerequisites consist of a tight story, good music, crisp conversation, excellent script and dialogues, fine acting by the lead roles, appropriate costumes, outstanding direction and careful editing. Then there was the matter of luck which remains undefined to this day. I have encountered films with excellent storylines that have turned out to be box-office flops. So while there is no exact formula for success, too much melodrama and a non-realistic storyline dooms a movie from the start.

My deep interest in films took me to the next level— assessing the acting abilities of the heroes and the skills of the director. Thus I gradually turned into a movie pundit.

Now I am unable to watch as many movies as I would like due to my schedule, yet, I prefer going to a movie theatre, rather than watching it at home.

I also have an interest in visiting countries that aren't considered popular tourist destinations. A few years ago, I added Iran, Poland, Cuba, the Bahamas, Uzbekistan and Iceland to the list. These less visited countries have many advantages.

They are not crowded and have fewer hotel reservations. The flight tickets to these places can be obtained at a short notice and you have the freedom to walk about anywhere you choose. Out of these four countries, the Bahamas was the most exotic of them all, even as I was introduced to the other countries and their specialties—whether it be their markets, vegetables, customs, cuisine, fashion and much more. I enjoy going to farmers' markets to sample the local goodies and always pick up something that I can carry around and eat.

During my visit to Iran, I was utterly fascinated to see yesteryear's Persia, especially since I was aware that we use almost 5000 Persian words in the local language of north Karnataka. The historical connection goes back to the days of the Adil Shahi dynasty. The official language in the court and the military was Persian. So it isn't surprising that many words and nuances of Persian architecture were absorbed by the locals in their language and can still be viewed in Bijapur and Bidar in Karnataka.

In the olden days, trade was an important part of administration and was responsible for bringing revenue into the kingdom. Many trader groups were in existence at that time, which enabled the exchange of goods from China to India and from India to the Western world. This also encouraged the sharing of culture through food, dance, theatre and cloth.

I decided to visit the local market in Shiraz, a prominent city, in an effort to better understand the culture and the type of merchandise and fare. At the market, I noticed a man busy making naans in a small stall and a few people waiting around for their order. The process was fascinating and the naans were ready to be served in a matter of a few minutes. When guests come home in Iran, women do not head to the kitchen and make rotis like we do in India. Instead, the man of the house goes to the naan and roomali roti (another type of thin flatbread) shop and gets them freshly made and in big quantities.

All the cooking made me feel hungry and I approached the man. 'I want to buy two of them,' I said in English.

It was clear that he wasn't too familiar with English, but he understood my request. Soon, he handed me two warm naans on a paper. I noticed him observing my sari and the bindi on my forehead.

Since I didn't know the cost, I offered him a higher denomination currency note so that he could charge me appropriately and return the change.

'Amitabh Bachchan?' he asked.

When I didn't respond, he persisted, 'Salman Khan? Shah Rukh Khan?'

After hearing the names of the famous Bollywood heroes, I realized what he was trying to say. 'Yes,' I replied. 'I am from the same country as them.'

He smiled. 'No money,' he said.

Even when I insisted, he refused. He added, 'India. Bollywood. Very nice. Good dance. Good dress. Good music. Iranian like.'

I understood. Iranians like Bollywood. Since I come from the same land as some of the heroes they like, the man didn't want to take any money from me. He wanted to give them to me as a gift. He probably thought of it as a way of doing something in return for the heroes' countrymen.

'Salaam!' His words broke through my train of thought and he moved on to the next client behind me.

I held those precious naans closely and came back to my room and turned the television on. To my pleasant surprise and amusement, I saw Amitabh Bachchan conversing in Persian with Jaya Bhaduri in the movie *Kabhi Khushi Kabhie Gham*. I had no doubt—Bollywood movies were definitely a rage in this country. The Iranians may not understand the meaning of the songs, but they must like our storylines, the beautiful and flowing silk lehengas, the foot-tapping music, the grandeur of the sets and the acting of the lead characters.

My next visit was to Havana, the capital of Cuba. The city is cut off from Western civilization and remains isolated from most of the world. The local language is Spanish and I couldn't say a single word except 'gracias' or thank you. To my surprise, there didn't seem to be any tourists from India. The weather was warm and there were beautiful sheltered markets that helped us escape the heat. The markets had almost everything possible on sale, including handicrafts, fruits and juices.

So with a glass of coconut water in hand, I wandered through the markets with my sister, who found a bag in a store filled with wooden and leather goods. As I helped her inspect the quality of the bag, she began to negotiate the price—a habit that is part of the Indian DNA, irrespective of one's financial position. Using her hands, the seller indicated the price—fifteen pesos. I noticed a young man standing by watching the interaction with obvious interest. Meanwhile, my sister instantly indicated ten without knowing the true value of the item she was buying. The seller came down to eleven pesos but my sister proudly refused to budge. The woman grinned, agreed and said something in Spanish. I heard the names Madhuri Dixit and Aamir Khan thrown in as the transaction finally took place.

Just when we were about to walk away, the young man on the side finally spoke. 'Do you know why that lady gave you the bag for only ten pesos?' he asked in broken English.

I shook my head.

'She says that she is a big fan of Aamir Khan and Madhuri Dixit. She wants you to tell them that they have fans in Havana and the rest of Cuba.'

I was surprised. 'Can you ask the seller where she sees their movies?'

The seller smiled when she heard the question and said something to the young man.

'She gets the DVDs,' he turned to me and said.

'Are they pirated?' I asked.

'I don't know,' he said. 'I can ask her if you want.'

I decided not to pursue the conversation since we couldn't communicate effectively. While I didn't get all my answers, it was clear that Bollywood enjoyed a big presence internationally, and that I had got a five-peso discount because of it!

I recalled one of my visits to Mumbai where I had met a new-age Indian actor–director and had an animated discussion about movies, of course!

'Bollywood is not just about cinema,' I said. 'If somebody talks about the importance of good values, it may impact one person in the crowd. If someone writes about them, then it may change a few more. But if it is shown in Bollywood through a powerful story, then the impact is much more drastic. As an actor, one must own the responsibility to spread the right messages.'

He agreed with me.

The influence of Bollywood is phenomenal indeed.

My travel adventures also took me to Bukhara, the fifth largest city of Uzbekistan. As I went for an evening stroll, the faint tunes of a familiar song *'Tujh Mein Rab Dikhta Hai'* wafted towards me. It was from the movie *Rab Ne Bana Di Jodi*. Just like the children who couldn't resist following the Pied Piper of Hamelin, my legs directed me towards the source of the music.

Within minutes, I found myself outside a restaurant by a pond—Lyabi House. As I attempted to enter, the doorman stopped me gently with a wave of his hand.

'I'm sorry, but the restaurant is at full capacity today and all our tables are occupied,' he said.

'But that song is mine!' I said, feeling as excited and proud as a six-year-old and pointing inside. 'I am from the country of that music!'

The doorman smiled and stepped aside to let me in.

Hurriedly, I entered the main room and walked right up to the singer, focused on his performance. By now, the music had changed and this time it was *'Tum Hi Ho'* from *Aashiqui 2*. 'I am from India and this song is from my country,' I said to him, the moment he stopped singing.

'Hindustan?' he asked.

I nodded.

'Namaste!' he grinned and nodded his head vigorously, as if to acknowledge what I had just said.

I looked around, and for the first time, I became aware of other people in the restaurant.

We tried to communicate quickly—he in Uzbek and I in Hindi with a spattering of as many Persian words that I could remember. We failed quite miserably.

Then he smiled and his melodious voice filled the air—'*Main Shayar To Nahi*'. The song must have been quite popular among the locals because suddenly there was a round of applause from the people in the room.

This wasn't about a big achievement such as a space mission or a sports victory, but about running into common people listening to a slice of India in an unknown corner of the world. My whole being felt a rush of mixed emotions—above everything else, a sense of pride that I belonged to a special country.

Even people in a country like England share their love for Bollywood dance. Indian restaurants are popular and are often based on the theme of Bollywood. Iceland also has a restaurant named Gandhi in Reykjavik. There is a statue of late Yash Chopra, a renowned Indian filmmaker, in Interlaken, Switzerland, and a poster of Shah Rukh Khan and Kajol at the entrance of Mount Titlis, a mountain of the Uri Alps.

Bollywood has also contributed to Hollywood's food dishes. There is a drink called Piggy Chops in Milk Bar, West

Hollywood, named after actress Priyanka Chopra, which consists of bananas, almonds, caramel sauce, vanilla ice cream and a splash of ginseng. Mallika Shake, on the other hand, is named after Mallika Sherawat and is a delicious mix of blueberries, blackberries, raspberries and strawberries, topped with chocolate sauce.

Young girls now want to dress like these heroines. I have seen several girls in my friend's boutique asking for dresses like the one Anushka Sharma wore in *Band Baaja Baaraat* or what Madhuri Dixit wore in *Hum Aapke Hain Kaun*.

Before my trip to Uzbekistan, I visited Iceland. I was a south Indian who wasn't used to wearing a sweater at any time of the year. Then how would I wear five layers of clothes? I must be the only crazy one wanting to visit the country, or so I thought. I was pretty sure that I wouldn't run into an Indian there because of the freezing temperatures.

When I finally reached the country for a prearranged tour, I met a nice local guide who greeted me in an accent I could barely understand. 'Do you want to see the locales of the "*Gerua*" song?' he asked.

I didn't understand a word and gazed at him in silence until he felt visibly uncomfortable. So he dug around in his bag and pulled out a DVD of the movie *Dilwale* starring Kajol and Shah Rukh Khan.

'Yes!' I exclaimed, as light dawned on me. I had seen the movie and had wondered where one of the song and dance sequences was shot.

On the way to Black Sand beach, he showed us the video of the song. The black pebbles and the floating icebergs took my breath away and we ended up spending a considerable amount of time there.

'We all love this song. It has made Iceland very popular with your countrymen and enhanced our tourism prospects,' he said.

As we headed back to the hotel, a Spanish fellow traveller next to me added, 'That is very true. We have benefited from Bollywood, too. The "Senorita" song from the movie *Zindagi Na Milegi Dobara* which was shot in Spain has made our country popular. The movie also brought the tomato festival to the limelight!'

I nodded. 'The movie has indeed made Spain a favoured holiday destination for Indians. We fancy the cities of Barcelona and Madrid and the La Tomatino festival. Somebody should consider giving an award to the movie's director Zoya Akhtar for enhancing the country's tourism income.'

I sat back and my mind wandered over the journey of Bollywood from black and white to colour movies, from Prithviraj Kapoor to Ranbir Kapoor, and from the touring talkies that operated for only three months a year to the movie-on-demand access that we have today.

Bollywood has graduated from being a part of the movie industry to becoming a vital partner when it comes to business generation. All in all, it is a great ambassador for our unique country.

9

Rasleela and the Swimming Pool

Harikatha is a traditional art form from the state of Karnataka wherein a narrator or *dasa*, along with a small troupe, goes from village to village and shares stories from the Hindu scriptures and epics. When they visited my village, Shiggaon, the audience eagerly assembled in the temple for an all-night performance. Multiple stories were depicted through dance and to the tunes of tamburas. The enactment was dependent solely on the expertise of the narrator and the dance.

One such evening, I accompanied my cousins to the Harikatha of Gopika Vastra Harana. The Harikatha dasa of this troupe was a well-known promoter named Gopinath who was known to portray stories from the Bhagavata Purana and deeply involve the audience. The stories would usually contain descriptions of Krishna's mischief, his mother's love and the cowherd girls' (or *gopikas'*) adoration.

That day, Gopinath began, 'Everybody, please close your eyes. Today is a warm day in the wondrous city of Vrindavan. Come, walk with me to the banks of the river Yamuna. The water is cold, the lotuses are blooming and the river flows lazily. Once we are there, just look around you. You will see beautiful gopikas sauntering along. What is the colour of their clothes?'

'Red and green!' a young girl said out loud.

'Yellow and orange,' said another.

'Now look at that big beautiful green tree near the river,' said Gopinath. 'The gopikas have changed into their bathing robes and left their dry clothes on the branches of the same tree. It is time for their bath and they get into the water and begin splashing each other. Now let's search for Krishna. Where do you think he is?'

'He's behind the kadamba tree,' someone shouted from the audience.

'He's next to Yashoda!' said another voice.

Gopinath continued, 'Let's approach Krishna. There he is—sitting on the high branch of a tree nearby and wasting his time.'

'Oh, he is such a prankster,' said a young girl from the troupe—one of the gopikas. 'But I like him. He brings a smile to my lips. My mother, however, gets upset because he takes away all the butter from our home.'

Then the troupe took over and the Harikatha continued.

A woman added, 'My mother-in-law has instructed me not to speak to Krishna because he drank all the milk in our house after entering through the back door.'

A voice complained, 'Whenever I take my pot to fetch water, he throws stones at it and breaks it. My husband is quite upset.'

'We must teach him a lesson,' insisted another from the troupe.

'Krishna overheard all of this,' interjected Gopinath, 'and stealthily hid their clothes. Once the gopikas had finished their bath in the river, they walked over to the tree but alas! Their clothes were nowhere to be found! How would they go back home in minimal and wet clothing? Who had stolen their clothes? Just then, they heard melodious tunes that seemed to originate from above them. When they looked up, they saw Krishna holding their clothes in one hand and playing the flute with the other, with his eyes closed. Of course! He must have heard them complaining and decided to take revenge. He wasn't going to return the clothes easily. So they began to plead with him. What did the women say?'

A girl from the audience yelled, 'O Krishna, please give back my sari.'

'And mine too!' shouted another. 'It's my favourite!'

The women began giving descriptions, with their eyes still shut.

'And that black sari with the red border is mine!'

'Oh, please, give me that green and mango-coloured sari!'

Gopinath was happy. 'Ah yes, all of you have seen Krishna now,' he said.

The conversations between Krishna and the gopikas and the audience continued until they raised their hands and surrendered, 'O Krishna! You are a kind-hearted boy and you understand our hearts. Please give us the saris. Otherwise we are left with no choice but to walk home in our wet robes. We are completely dependent on you.'

'Krishna smiled and started throwing down the clothes,' said Gopinath. 'The gopikas wore their saris and after they were well-clothed, Krishna descended from the top and the dancing began.'

The sounds of music and dance filled the air and the night ended on a joyful note. The Harikatha dasa told us to open our eyes. That's when we found out that two and a half hours had passed.

As a young girl, I had a vivid imagination. It was easy to visualize the flow of the river Yamuna, the pink lotuses, the bright and colourful gopikas, Lord Krishna and his naughty but compassionate face, and the music floating from his flute. I was enchanted!

Years later, I went to Vrindavan. To my utter disappointment, the Yamuna was dirty and more of a rivulet than a full-bodied river. The place was now commercialized.

Almost all the priests I observed were directing the devotees to a tree with pieces of cloth tied to it. 'Lord Krishna sat on this tree and threw the clothes down to the gopikas,' they said.

Devotees bowed to the tree and tied a small piece of cloth to it.

The image was not what I had associated with the story. So I closed my eyes and turned away. 'I don't want to see this and ruin my childhood images,' I thought.

I also realized in my adulthood that a story such as this might be considered harassment in the modern world. But the truth is that such a concept did not exist in the olden days. God is considered to be an omnipotent friend—someone who is approachable and whom we can speak to at any time and anyhow we choose. These tales are meant to bring out the human side of the Lord, while retaining the devotion towards him. So he is depicted as a naughty young lad, no more than eight years old, who enjoys spending time with his devotees and teasing them with love and innocence. This is why the women also play along until they completely surrender to the Lord—a gesture of faith after which he gives them whatever they need.

Decades later, I became a grandmother to two little girls—Krishna and Anoushka. When they grew from toddlers to young children, I decided to share some of my childhood stories with them. I thought that they would visualize the scenes just like I had.

One day, when I was playing with them in their residence in London, they asked me for a story. I told them the same tale of Lord Krishna and the gopikas. Since I had their attention, I added the story of *Akshaya Patra* too.

'Draupadi was very hospitable and entertained many guests when she was living in Indraprastha. Unfortunately, due to a turn of events, she had to accompany her husbands on a long exile and felt sad that she could no longer take care of the guests like she used to.

'Her husband, Yudhishthira, prayed to the sun god, Surya, and explained their difficulty in taking care of the guests. So Surya blessed them and handed them a vessel. "This is a special vessel known as Akshaya Patra," he said.

"You can use this to feed as many people as you want. But on one condition . . ."

'"What's that?" asked Yudhishthira.

'"You can't cook any food after the lady of the house has eaten. The vessel can be used again only after the next sunrise."

'Yudhishthira nodded.

'Happily, Draupadi began feeding her visitors with different varieties of food.

'Soon, the news of her pleasing hospitality reached Duryodhana's ears, who felt jealous despite the fact that his cousins were in exile and led a much humbler life than they were used to. A few days later, the short-tempered sage Durvasa arrived at Duryodhana's palace and was treated as an esteemed guest and given all that could be offered.

'Pleased, he blessed Duryodhana. "I am happy with your hospitality towards me and my disciples. Ask me whatever you want and I will fulfil your wish."

'Duryodhana and his evil uncle, Shakuni, had already pre-decided what they would ask for, should Durvasa give them such an opportunity.

'He smiled. "My cousins, the Pandavas, are devout and pious," said Duryodhana, pretending to care for them. "I will be grateful if you could bless them too. If you leave now, you will reach there late in the evening. That is all I want."

'Durvasa agreed and set out with his group.

'On the surface, the request was a simple one and seemed to show the largeness of Duryodhana's heart, but the truth was far from it. Shakuni and Duryodhana knew that by the time Durvasa and his disciples reached the Pandavas' home, Draupadi would have finished her meal and the Pandavas wouldn't be able to feed all of them. This would immediately fuel the sage's wrath, who was then highly likely to curse them.

'After a journey that took many hours, Durvasa reached the Pandavas' abode and said to them, "Your cousin Duryodhana is an excellent host. He has requested me to experience your hospitality too and bless you. My disciples and I will first go for a bath in the river nearby. Please have our food ready for us by the time we return."

'The moment Durvasa left, Yudhishthira rushed into the kitchen and to his dismay, saw Draupadi washing and cleaning the Akshaya Patra. "Draupadi! Durvasa will soon come here with his students for a meal and you have already eaten yours! I don't want to get on his bad side. What should we do?"

'Sunset was fast approaching and Draupadi was at a loss. Unable to think of a solution, her thoughts turned to Krishna, who was as good as a brother to her. Just then, she heard the sound of horses and a chariot pulling up outside the home. She walked towards the entrance but within seconds, Krishna walked in through the open door.

'When he saw Draupadi and the rest of the Pandavas with long faces, he asked, "Why are you all so sad?"

'Yudhishthira explained the situation to him. "Bring the vessel to me," said Krishna.

'With reluctance, Draupadi fetched the Akshaya Patra, "There's nothing there, brother. See for yourself."

'"Sister, you may be a queen but you are definitely not a good cleaner. Look at this—you have left a grain of rice."

'Krishna picked up the grain, ate it and burped rather loudly. "I am happy and my stomach is full. May God bless you," he said and immediately left before the Pandavas could stop him.

'Meanwhile, Durvasa and his students were finishing their bath in the river when they suddenly felt as if they had just had a full meal. Their stomachs felt extremely full and satisfied.

'They looked at each other. "Sir," a student gathered his courage and spoke to Durvasa. "We are feeling full and can't eat any more. Let's skip the visit to the Pandavas' home because we won't be able to eat anything and that might offend them."

'Durvasa smiled and said, "Yes, my children, I understand how you feel. While there is no end to greed in life, hunger is one thing that has its limitation. Once you are full, no matter what you say or do, you just can't force yourself to eat. I will bless the Pandavas from here and we can leave."'

Once the story had ended, both Krishna and Anoushka looked at my face.

'Now that I have told you two stories today, you must think about them and repeat them to me tomorrow!' I said.

The two girls waltzed their way to their room, discussing the last story with each other.

I was happy that I had taught them two important mythological stories in a very simple manner.

The next morning after breakfast, Krishna came and sat next to me. 'Ajji,' she said. 'I have changed a little bit of your story.'

'Tell me then.'

Anoushka also joined us and Krishna began, 'Krishna was a cute little boy who was very naughty. He would frequently visit his friends' homes, open the fridge without permission and eat whatever he wanted to. This upset the mothers and yet everybody was fond of him.'

'He took pizzas, pastas, sandwiches, cheese, butter, yogurt, fruits and everything that caught his fancy,' added Anoushka and giggled.

'Be quiet! I am the one telling the story,' said Krishna. 'It was the Christmas season and all schools were closed. One day, the girls and their mothers decided to meet at the indoor swimming pool. Once they were there, they changed into their swimwear, kept the clothes in the lockers, left the keys on one of the benches in the changing room, showered and jumped into the pool.

'Soon they were in the heated pool splashing around, despite the freezing temperatures outside.

'What they didn't know was that Krishna was also there. He saw the girls from the first floor and opened the window overlooking the pool.

'The girls were talking about him. "Oh, Krishna is so adorable but he troubles me," said one of them. "The other day he ate my cookies but I didn't complain to anyone."

'"Oh, he steals my pencils so often!"

'"Your pencils? He takes my toys!" another girl whined.

'"We must inform the headmistress."

'Krishna heard the comments, went to the changing room, found the locker keys and slipped away.

'After the swim, the girls and the mothers showered and went to gather their clothes from the lockers. But the keys were missing!

'"Who has taken our keys?" they asked the staff.

'"Ma'am, only girls are allowed here at this time of the day. Nobody else can enter."

'"But we are miserable, cold and wet," said one of the mothers. "How will we go home?"

'"My new shoes are also in the locker!" a girl yelled.

'"I have a birthday party to attend after this and my dress is inside the locker! What should I do now?"

'The attendant didn't know what to do. "Give me a few minutes. Let me speak to the manager," she said.

'Suddenly, the tunes from a harmonica floated towards them. They looked towards the source of the beautiful music and saw Krishna on the first floor patio almost right above them. There was a bunch of keys dangling from one of his fingers.

'Once he realized that they had seen him, he stopped playing the harmonica. "Girls, if you complain about me to the headmistress, none of you will get your clothes back."

'"We will sue you!" said a girl.

'"You can sue me all you want, but you can't go anywhere without your clothes. After all, it is snowing outside!"

'"O Krishna, we are very sorry," said the girls in unison.

'"If we wanted to complain, we would have already done so. You are dear to us and we love your pranks! You know that it's the truth. So stop this. We will catch a cold standing here like this. You don't want us to fall sick, do you?" said one of the more logical girls.

'Krishna smiled and threw the keys to the girls. Then they all got dressed and went with Krishna to the nearest café for a hot chocolate.' My granddaughter ended her story.

Anoushka clapped loudly and laughed. She had enjoyed the story!

I nodded to show my appreciation. The truth was that I was completely unprepared for this new variation of the story that seemed to be set in London. The old story made me visualize the river Yamuna, its cold water, the floating lotuses and a flute-playing Krishna but this urban version of the Lord was too hard for me to relate to!

Hesitantly, I turned to Anoushka. What version of the second story would I hear next?

Right on cue, Anoushka started, 'Draupadi was a beautiful and powerful queen. One day, she left the city and decided to stay in a village far away. She drank clear water from the stream, picked organic food directly from the trees and plants and cooked for all the guests who came home. However, the food was insufficient sometimes. She explained this problem to her husband, Yudhishthira, who, in turn, shared the issue with a friend, Surya.

'Surya was very resourceful. He gifted Yudhishthira and Draupadi a special cooker and some additives. He said, "Whenever you make rice in this, add these healthy additives. Two spoons of this cooked rice will be enough for one person. You won't have to cook large quantities or spend hours in search of food. But Draupadi, once you eat, clean the vessel and don't cook in it again that day. This will keep the bacteria away and ensure that the food remains hygienic. So be careful about the way you use it."

'Draupadi nodded. From that day on, she made the special organic rice for her guests.

'One day, her uncle came without informing her, with many people in tow. He said, "Draupadi, I have heard that you make tasty rice. I want to try that today. My group and I will go for a swim first and then come back for the delicious meal."

'Draupadi was upset. First, her uncle hadn't informed her in advance and second, he simply showed up on their doorstep with so many others to feed! Besides, she had already eaten and cleaned the vessel. She was about to give her uncle a piece of her mind but Yudhishthira stopped her. "Uncle has helped us many times, dear wife. Please don't say anything to him. You know how short-tempered he is! Let's not do anything that we will regret later."

'Draupadi was worried. How would she feed so many people now? She immediately called her brother Krishna who was kind, helpful and a strategic thinker. He came to her assistance and asked her to show him the vessel. He took the last grain of rice stuck at the corner of the vessel and ate it.

'"Hmm, the rice is indeed very tasty but I am sure that your uncle and the other guests will not come back for it."

'"Why?" asked Draupadi.

'"They know why," he said with a mysterious smile and left for an appointment.

'Meanwhile, at the swimming pool, each member of the group swallowed a little bit of the chlorine water. Since the chlorine level was high that day, all of them soon began feeling uncomfortable and kept running to the bathroom. Finally, Uncle said to the group, "I think we have all fallen sick and are low on energy at the moment. Let us not go to Draupadi's home for the big meal. It is best to give our stomachs a little break."

'The group murmured in agreement.

'So Uncle called Draupadi on her cell phone and said, "My dear child, please excuse us. We will not be able to eat at your home today. I promise we will come another time."

'Draupadi smiled. As always, her brother had come to her rescue! "You are always welcome here, Uncle, but please let me know in advance next time," she said and hung up.'

I was stumped. The stories had been transformed, and how! After that reinvention, I didn't have the guts to share the story of Draupadi's disrobing in the royal court!

10

A Day in Infosys Foundation

Shoba is one of my school friends. In a small town like Hubli, it is common for close friends to become as comfortable with each other as siblings. As life usually turns out, we walked down different paths and Shoba settled down in Hubli, while I moved to Bengaluru. Her children, like many others in Karnataka, became software engineers and moved to Bengaluru. So Shoba frequented the city to visit her children and often called on me whenever possible.

One day, she phoned my office. Since I was in a meeting, I passed on a message to her that I would call her back later. When I reached out to her in the evening, she asked, 'Why did you take so long to return my call?'

'Shoba, I got time to return my personal calls just a short while ago.'

'I know that you are very busy,' she said, sounding a little concerned. 'But it's so difficult to reach you when I want to—sometimes you are at work or travelling or out for an appointment even during the hours when I think you might be at home. I only wanted to invite you for my grandson's first birthday. It is on Monday and you must come at whatever time is convenient for you.'

'Oh Shoba! It is almost impossible for me to visit you on a working day, especially Monday.'

'Can't you spare one hour for a close friend?' asked Shoba, the way only old friends can do. 'I know that you are the chairperson of a foundation and you must be having visitors all the time asking you for grants, but you can always reschedule or refuse to meet them. They will come again, I'm sure!'

'It isn't that simple,' I replied. 'With the two hours that takes from Jayanagar to your home and back, half my day will be gone. A day at the foundation is filled with many activities, some of which aren't easy to explain. For someone who doesn't work there, it may appear to be the apparent simple task of giving money or grants. If you really want to know what I do, then come and shadow me for a day. Maybe then you will get a glimpse into the complicated nature of social work.'

Enthusiastically, Shoba agreed and a few weeks later, on a Monday, she joined me for a day at the office.

I was happy that she had come. I told her, 'You will only observe and not comment or participate as I go about my day! Is that okay?'

She smiled and nodded.

Meanwhile, I gave my assistant, Asha, a list of people with whom I needed to speak to that morning. Soon, the phone rang. Asha sprang into action and answered the call.

A voice spoke, 'We are from Hubli and know Mrs Sudha Murty very well. I'd like to speak with her.'

'What is your name, madam?'

'Usha. Usha Patil.'

Asha turned to me, 'Usha Patil is on the line. May I connect her to you?'

Usha is a common name in Hubli and so is the last name Patil. I knew at least ten Usha Patils from Hubli—a neighbour, a classmate, a cousin, a cousin's wife, a writer, an acquaintance, a temple priest's daughter and a few more and I wondered who this person was.

Asha seemed to be at a loss, just like me.

I took the phone from Asha. 'Sudha Murty here,' I said.

'I am Usha Patil from Kundgol, a village near Hubli. My son needs a job . . .'

'Do I know you?'

'No, but you are from Hubli. That's why I am sure that you will help someone from there.'

'Usha ji, why did you say that you know me?'

'I do know you through newspapers and television,' she justified. 'But I didn't say that you knew me. Keeping that aside, my son is keen on getting employed soon.'

I was firm. 'I am not responsible for recruiting people at Infosys. Please email the human resources department for this as they have their own procedure.'

'But if you put in a word, they won't refuse your request,' she persisted.

'I'm sorry, Usha ji, but this is a matter of hiring professionals and employees are hired only after interviews and tests. I run the foundation and don't interfere with the process of another department.'

Usha wasn't convinced. She sounded reluctant. 'Then will you give me the details of an appropriate contact?'

'You can send the resume via email,' I replied.

'Please hold on for a moment while I find a pen and take down the email address.'

I didn't have time to wait and gave the phone back to Asha, 'Give her the recruitment email address and from now on, when someone says that they know me well, please also ask if I know them.'

I went and sat down to check my emails.

Leena, my secretary, said, 'Madam, there are 410 emails for you today.'

The number was not unusual. 'Let's separate it based on its category and then start from the bottom.'

Once that was done, we began. The first was an email describing me as if I were some kind of a goddess. 'Leena, just read the last line,' I said.

'The request is for a grant to build a temple,' Leena explained.

The foundation does not help with any religious constructions or restorations unless it is of archaeological importance, as declared by the state or central government. 'Please send our regrets,' I said.

By the time Leena and I moved to the next email, most of the cell phones began chiming in the office indicating that we had received several messages. They were all in response to one that said, 'Infosys Foundation is giving scholarships to all those who apply. Contact the foundation immediately.'

The phones also began ringing.

The news was absolutely untrue. Several years ago, the foundation had offered limited scholarships, but the programme had been terminated based on the exit policy at the end of the specified term. Despite this, we were aware that some people were floating this information on the instant messaging application WhatsApp. As a result, students and parents often inundated us with emails, letters and phone calls.

I asked Asha to reply to each query in the same mode that it was received. I knew it would keep Asha busy for a few hours.

Once that was done, Leena and I opened the second email. A university wanted to confer an honorary doctorate on me.

Leena was thrilled but I wasn't. Soon enough, we read the relevant line, 'Once you receive the doctorate, you will become an alumnus, and we are sure that you will help the university in any way that you can.'

I scratch your back and you scratch mine. 'Please decline the doctorate politely,' I told Leena.

The next request was an invitation to be the chief guest for a college's annual day in Mumbai. While I usually can't go to most of the events that come my way, I make an effort to attend at least a few. Leena told me that the event was only for two hours but the travel time to Mumbai and back would take one and a half days. I considered declining it, but then thought of the students, who I always hold dear.

'If I am going to Mumbai that day for work, I will attend it,' I said.

She checked my diary. 'You are going to be in Mumbai for meetings in the afternoon on that date and there are a few available hours in the morning. Luckily, the venue is close to the airport and you can go there after you land. We can reschedule the flight and you can leave early in the morning from Bengaluru.'

'Tell the college management that I will be there slightly early at 9.30 a.m. and must depart by 11 a.m.'

The shrill ringing of the phone on my desk interrupted our conversation and Asha immediately took the call, 'Hello?'

A few seconds later, she handed me the phone, 'Kasab is on the line.'

I was frightened. At the time, Kasab was a Pakistani militant convicted for the Taj hotel bombing on 26/11 in Mumbai. As far as I knew, he had been executed. But sometimes nothing is as it seems. 'Was he really calling me? And why?'

I told Asha to give me a minute to gather my thoughts and to inform Kasab that I would speak with him.

She spoke to him briefly and turned to me. 'Kasab is very angry. He's saying that he's a patriotic citizen and is asking me why I am addressing him in this manner.'

I was confused. 'What did you say to him, Asha?'

'I called the number from the list you gave me earlier in the morning and told him to hold while I transferred the call to your phone.'

'I never gave you Kasab's number nor did I ask you to call someone by that name. Kasab is dead and gone. Do you even know who he was?'

'I don't know,' she replied casually, least bothered about the affairs of the state.

'Give me the phone.'

I could hear a man fuming on the other end.

'Hello?' I said.

'My grandfather was a freedom fighter and I have served the country as an ex-MLA. I am proud of my heritage. How dare you call me Kasab?'

I sighed. Asha had called Kasabe and mispronounced his name to sound like that of the notorious terrorist. It was an absolute dishonour and an insult to a true patriot.

'I am extremely sorry for the confusion, sir.' I apologized. 'This is Sudha Murty. I told my staff to call you so that I could inform you that I won't be able to come for the wedding as I have to travel on the same day. But I will visit your home on my way to the airport.'

Hearing my voice, Kasabe calmed down. After I disconnected the call, I turned to my assistant, 'Why did you call him Kasab?'

'Madam, there were three phones ringing at the same time. I thought I called him Kasabe, maybe he misheard it. Why will I call him a different name on purpose?'

Meanwhile, the office manager, Krishnamurthy, approached me and said, 'Madam, the payment vouchers are ready.'

Our office is cashless and so are its transactions. This policy turned out to be a boon during the demonetization of currency in 2016 as we were relatively unaffected.

Prashant, the CSR manager, interrupted us, 'Did you promise a matching grant to our employees' non-profit arm during your recent visit to Chandigarh?'

'Yes, I did,' I replied. 'It is a good way to involve them in some of our CSR efforts and will inspire them to pool in money for some of the activities. I have encouraged this in other development centres too, such as Hyderabad, Pune, Mangalore, Thiruvananthapuram, Chennai and Bhubaneswar.'

Prashant's forehead creased with obvious worry. 'We are overshooting the allocated funds for this year. It doesn't match with our plan for the year. Please review our latest budget.'

I understood his concern. Prashant monitored the finances and kept a close eye on the budget.

'We will manage it. It is better to have deserving projects in the pipeline than to worry about the budget. We can request for more money if needed. There are projects that may get delayed or aren't ready yet, so there is no need to worry.'

Since I was once a professor, I often talk like a teacher to everyone in my office. Most of the time, Prashant and Shrutee, the program director, end up being the target of my wisdom-sharing talks because they are responsible for the annual balance sheets and reaching our CSR goals.

Despite my regular interventions, they were often apprehensive when our commitments exceeded the finances in hand.

The next phone call was from the management of the Bannerghatta National Park for a grant update.

During the past summer, we had learnt that the animals there suffered from an acute shortage of drinking water. The authorities had constructed a tub for the tigers to sit in but the water had to be changed every few days to avoid infection and disease. Tigers were difficult to treat when they were unwell and hence, the caretakers were always wary about the water. So I called one of our contractors and instructed him to dig borewells in accessible areas and also construct an overhead water tank. Many tried to dissuade us due to the lack of water in the area but we went ahead anyway. We had to try for the sake of the animals.

The call was to inform us that there was plenty of water in the borewells. The animals would finally get enough good quality water and remain free from diseases as much as possible. I thanked God for this great gesture.

I glanced at Leena. She was still busy sorting the emails into various categories such as travel, pending, appointments, regrets and new initiatives.

Everyone was immersed in their work. At times, I feel like I do not have much to do as most of it is appropriately handled. Only a few new proposals, exceptions or escalations usually come my way.

It was time for Shrutee's appointment with a visitor. She went upstairs to the conference room for the meeting while I began scanning the snail mail kept for me even as the phones kept ringing.

After a few minutes, one of our contractors called for an urgent update. 'Madam,' he said, 'some workers went on holiday a week ago and haven't returned yet. If we have to work with the existing workers alone, the project will be delayed by one month.'

'You can't do this!' I protested. 'I have already invited the chief minister for the inauguration and everything has been planned. You must finish it somehow.'

'Madam, please, then tell me what to do.'

I didn't know what he could do, but kept insisting that he should complete the work faster. After a long discussion, he agreed to hasten his work and delay by only fifteen days. It would be right on time for the inauguration. Experience has taught me that delays happen in most construction works, no matter how good a person is in project management, and hence I allowed some leeway.

Just then, Shrutee requested me to join her for the meeting. 'I have communicated our decision regarding the proposal,' she said. 'But the team wants to meet you. There are three of them. I think it's better to meet them or else they will definitely visit again.'

At Infosys Foundation, we have our own strategies and policies. For instance, we don't approve grants for political parties and no consideration is given to caste, creed or religion during proposal reviews. There is an exit policy, an internal and external audit and a third-party assessment for every project, and we are inclined towards releasing money in instalments.

The project wasn't a good fit for us and hence Shrutee had chosen to decline it.

Here at the foundation, we believe that if we are refusing a proposal, then we must communicate it as soon as possible. *Adinishtura* is better than *antyanishtura*, which means that an initial disappointment is better than a disagreement at the end.

'Okay, I will come,' I said and accompanied her upstairs.

Most people insist on meeting me. A few think that if they put pressure on me directly, I might give in, but they don't know the truth—Shrutee and I are always on the same page.

But I decided to meet the visitors to help Shrutee. Just as I expected, they elaborated on the merits of their proposal for the next thirty minutes. In the end, I said, 'Providing grants is not akin to approving whatever we feel like. Please understand that there are certain systems and processes in place here. Shrutee has communicated the right decision and unfortunately, we will not be able to be a part of this.'

They were upset, but nothing further could be done at this point.

There are times when the company directors forward us letters and requests that come to them. We evaluate them objectively and reject or approve them. I thank the management for never pressuring us or influencing the process.

It was time for lunch. Since my house was nearby, I said to Shoba, 'Let's go eat and come back soon.'

At home, a security guard informed me that my daughter, Akshata, had called.

When I called her back, she threw a flurry of questions at me. 'Where were you yesterday? Are you unwell? Or has something happened there that you aren't telling me? I have been so worried.'

I was surprised by her tone. 'I am right here in Bengaluru. I was attending meetings all day. Why are you worried?'

'When I spoke to the security staff yesterday in the morning, they said that you were in the toilet. When I phoned in the afternoon, they again said that you were in the toilet. It was the same story in the evening and later at night, they said that you were sleeping. This morning, they said that you had left for office. I sent you an email but didn't hear back. Why were you in the restroom all day?'

She sounded anxious.

Calmly, I said, 'Breathe, Akshata! Do some pranayama every day. I had gone for a site visit to check the status of our recently inaugurated toilets. This was followed by other meetings and a panel discussion on how to construct them. I told the security staff that I was going for the toilet project work and maybe he misunderstood it and only remembered the word toilet. Don't be so afraid! As for your email, I haven't seen it yet as it has been a busy day!'

I could hear an immediate sigh of relief.

After hanging up, I went to the main gate and asked the security guard there, 'Didn't I inform all of you that I would be back late because of the toilet project?'

'I wasn't on duty, madam. Yesterday's guard has an ear infection and has taken the day off.'

Well, that explained the guard's inability to hear the day before. But I sure spent a lot of time in the toilet! I smiled to myself and went back inside.

During lunch, my cook and I began making the grocery list. He wanted to know the number of people coming home for dinner and the menu for the night. My mind, however, was still in office matters and it was difficult to make the sudden switch to the domestic conversation. I said, 'Let's talk about it later in the evening. Till then, just make what you can with whatever is available.'

After a quick lunch, Shoba and I returned to the office.

My next appointment was one that had been put off a long time ago. At first, all the three men who came spoke together and I couldn't understand anything. So I asked them to speak one at a time.

'I have received many awards in this area of work,' said the first.

The second one added, 'And I have the political connections to make things happen.'

'Let me first tell you why we have come here and how we will help the urban poor through the drinking water project,' said the third.

'Please allow me to ask you a few questions,' I said gently. 'Have you gone to the proposed area where you intend to work? And if so, what is the distribution of the population and the ratio of the number of males to the number of females?'

The three fell silent.

I changed the line of questioning. 'Where will you get the supply of drinking water from?'

No response.

'Is there an existing system in place that doesn't work? And if so, why not?' I tried again.

With no answers in sight, I gave up. 'Please prepare a well-researched proposal and execution plan with all these answers. After that, we will discuss it at the next internal review. If you give me the details of the location, I will make a personal visit there,' I said. 'It really doesn't matter who is ruling the area politically or who will bestow awards upon us. We specifically target the underprivileged and hope to help them through our efforts and see them smile.'

The three men seemed disappointed, most likely because I hadn't committed any funds for their project.

While I was saying goodbye, there was a knock on the door and Leena came in. 'Madam, you have to reconsider your travel plans. In your absence last week, I received many phone calls from all over the country for project visits in different locations. We have to allocate the site visits between Prashant, Shrutee and you. I need some of your time to block the dates today.'

I glanced at the calendar in the room. 'Fix my tours for the weekends so I can continue with my routine work on weekdays. If I have to visit Delhi, then plan all my project visits around the region, including places like Jammu and Lucknow, at the same time. I want to avoid unnecessary trips as much as possible.'

Leena nodded and went back with a determined glint in her eye. She would figure out the jigsaw puzzle of my travel plans herself.

I made my way to my room. All the emails had been sorted and directed to the appropriate people. I went through the ones left for me and began responding to them.

Next, I switched over to the physical mails. One of my goals is to have a paperless office, but I don't see it happening any time soon. We still receive hard copies of brochures, request letters and invitations.

Since I am an author, I receive many complimentary books too. It is a running joke that the number of authors exceeds the number of readers these days. Some of the writers request for a foreword, others want me to promote their books by stocking them in libraries and schools, and a few want to know my opinion on their books. Some authors send us their original manuscripts and ask us to send it back, which causes unnecessary hassles. The books for libraries are handed over to a selection committee, while the foreword and opinion requests are declined most of the time due to my tight schedule. By evening, our trash bins are usually full.

Then there are letters from my readers to the foundation office. These are a mixed bag—some share their experiences, some criticize certain aspects of my writing while others appreciate it. I take these home to answer during my personal hours.

My task was interrupted by a call from a news channel. The journalist asked me, 'What is your opinion on the current government? What are your thoughts about the demonetization of currency and its execution?'

I declined to comment. I may be good at what I do but I had no expertise in such matters.

I began sifting through the letters, some of which I routed to Leena for a suitable reply. There was a bunch of letters from the families of army martyrs thanking the foundation for our small contribution. Two others caught my attention—one was from the central government and another from the state government. Both were reaching out to the foundation to seek help for some projects. These were added to the agenda for the next week's internal review.

Leena came in to give me an update. 'Madam, I have worked out your travel plans. You will be travelling fifteen days a month for the next three months. Besides losing most of the weekends, you will also miss your distant niece's wedding and your father's death anniversary. Is that okay?'

'That's fine, Leena. Thank you. My father has taught me that work is worship and I know that he would understand if he was here.'

Leena handed over my travel details to Krishnamurthy, who immediately started arranging my tickets and accommodation at the company guesthouses wherever possible. Staying at the guesthouses allows easier coordination of my plans and also allows us to save money that we would otherwise have to spend on hotels.

Minutes later, Shrutee came by. 'I have some good news,' she said. 'The boys whom we supported in the Mathematics Olympiad have got admission in MIT and Caltech. In their media interview, they thanked the foundation profusely and said that our small gift of ten thousand rupees towards their effort pushed them to choose science. There is also an email from Pavagada. The selfless swamiji who works for blind children has written that the midday meal programme has been successful in making the children stay in school. The donation for their music classes has also made them happy. They even received an award recently. He has sent pictures of their bright little faces smiling with pride.'

Once she left, I sat in silence for a few minutes.

The loud ringing of the phone jolted me out of my thoughts. Out of instinct, I picked up the phone but Leena was already on the other extension with the caller. The person was screaming at Leena, 'I deserve more money from the foundation than what they have given me. You are only a secretary. Connect me to your boss and tell them who I am. If you don't, I will go to the media and tell them about the foundation. So be careful before you respond.'

I immediately went to Leena in the next room and took the phone from her.

'Sir, what is the problem?' I asked.

'I requested for two crores for a school but you have given us two lakhs—it is a pittance for the foundation. I want . . . no, I demand an explanation. I am an influential activist and can tarnish the name of the foundation if I want to.'

'Sure. I will give you an explanation. We get more than a hundred genuine applications and around two hundred calls every day. We don't work under any sort of pressure nor do we care to gain any advantage from our grants. There is an established process in place and we have to distribute the grants to the best of our judgement. We do not increase our grants without a review of the progress made. Experience has taught us that the work speaks for itself. Besides, there are trustees who are also involved with the decision-making. We may not be there in the foundation at a future date, but the established processes will continue. I must also tell you that we aren't afraid of the media because we haven't done anything wrong or under wraps.'

The man calmed down and cleared his throat. 'Well, if we do well and clear the review, then will you help us next year?'

'Maybe. We help many organizations and are not afraid of approaching the good ones ourselves. It is the quality of work that attracts us and we do not worry about potential threats or the connections of our beneficiaries.'

I could hear a murmur that vaguely seemed to sound like an apology.

I had had a hard day and was in no mood to let him off the hook. 'Sir, we also have difficult days at the foundation but we try to ensure that it does not affect our relationships with others,' I gave advice that nobody asked me for.

A glance at the clock confirmed that it was almost 5.30 p.m. I was planning to stay back a little longer but Shoba stood up from the chair nearby.

'I think I will leave,' she said.

I walked with her till the main gate to see her off. On the way, she passed the reception, where we had displayed some of our awards.

'Are you proud of all these?' she asked and pointed at the awards.

'In my younger days, I was. As the years passed and my experience grew, I realized that my joy was coming from the work and not from these occasional awards. Today, they don't matter much to me personally but they are important to my organization.'

'Tell me, why do you continue to give your remaining years to this thankless job?' she asked. 'You can sit back, relax, spend time with your grandchildren, go to weddings and birthdays and reduce a little bit of stress from your life.'

'The truth is that I am the luckiest of them all. I love what I do and every day is a holiday for me because of it. Who doesn't love a vacation?' I grinned.

Shoba smiled as she got into the car and nodded. I waved goodbye and went back to work.

11

I Can't, We Can

Recently, I attended a nephew's wedding. It was a wonderful occasion to meet my cousins whom I had spent my childhood with but hadn't met in a long time. The wedding ceremony began and a few cousins and I sat leisurely in a corner.

One of my cousins said, 'I am the president of the laughing club in our community. Come for one of our sessions. We hardly meet any more. This way I will at least get to see you for some time!'

It is common now to see older men and women gather in parks in the morning and attempt to laugh—ha ha ha. I have often wondered how people can make themselves laugh in this manner! I visualized myself attending such an assembly. What would I talk to them about? I was absolutely clueless and so I politely declined.

Another cousin said, 'I am the secretary of the housewives' association in my apartment community. I have already shared with the members that you are my cousin. You must come and address them.'

'But what is the subject matter that you are interested in?'

'You are a wise investor. So give the women tips on how to save and identify high-return investments like you have.'

'I'm not sure I understand. Can you elaborate a little on that?'

'Well, everybody knows how you invested ten thousand rupees in Infosys and made millions in return.'

'I didn't do that for the sake of investment,' I said in a serious tone. 'I gave the seed money to fulfil my husband's dream—a dream that was considered impractical in those days. He is successful now and that's why you are referring to me as a wise millionaire. Had he not been so, you would have called the same move a foolish one. You have it all wrong—I am not the right person to talk about investment. Instead, you can ask me for advice on how to spend money. That will be more suited to my skills!'

People around me laughed.

'I have a special request,' a third cousin said. She began, 'My friend's daughter is a bright student and . . .'

'Is she planning to apply for a job at Infosys?' I interrupted her. 'Because I really can't . . .'

'Have some patience,' she stopped me. 'Let me finish. I thought you would have garnered a lot more patience by now, considering your line of work. The girl wants your guidance. She already has a job offer as well as an admission letter from an American university, and needs to pick one.'

'There's not much guidance I can give. The decision depends on the family's financial position, the girl's ambition and her career plans, along with other social aspects of the family.'

'Come on! Meet her. She really needs your help.'

I was reluctant. But I said, 'Okay, ask her to meet me tomorrow at 9 a.m. She can come to my office.'

The next morning, I met the young petite girl named Jaya. She was shy and quite nervous.

I wanted to make her comfortable, so I told her to sit down and offered her a cup of tea. Then I asked for her mark sheet. Her academic record was outstanding. 'Jaya, what's on your mind?' I did not beat around the bush. 'Where do you see yourself in ten years?'

She was quiet.

I rephrased my question, 'Perhaps you want to be a corporate professional or pursue the academic line? Or maybe something else?'

Still, there was no reply.

'Are you scared of me? Do I look like a monster?' I persisted and smiled.

She smiled back and shook her head. Then she began speaking very softly about her future plans.

I could see that she didn't have any confidence, despite her achievements.

'Jaya, academic excellence is not everything,' I said. 'You must have confidence in yourself. One of the flaws of our education system is that it doesn't really teach us that quality. Our parents, society and the recruitment process concentrate too much on the marks we get. I can give you many examples of people who may not have studied much but have done well for themselves because they believed they could. Confidence doesn't mean that everything will go our way. It simply gives us the ability to accept failures that we will inevitably meet on our path and move forward with hope.'

Without any warning, Jaya started sobbing. Like a toddler. It was heartbreaking.

At first, I was startled. 'Maybe I have given her too strong a dose without knowing her nature,' I thought. In India, most of us excel at giving advice without people asking for it, and I am no exception.

I offered her a tissue and said, 'I am sorry if I have hurt you, Jaya. But I don't know what to tell you. You aren't sharing much with me.'

The girl calmed down and wiped her tears. Her voice was shaking when she spoke, 'No, ma'am, your advice didn't make me cry. The truth is that I feel inferior in front of most people.'

'Why? Anyone in your shoes would be proud of accomplishing so much at your age.'

She paused. Then she said, 'Ma'am, my father was an alcoholic.'

I paused.

She spoke a little more fluently, 'He is now in AA but my younger years were different. He would often get drunk and abuse my mother. She went through so much, and I had no idea what I could do to help her. I grew up scared of my father's temper and in an unhappy and tense atmosphere. Then I thought that the only way I could make a change was to study hard and get a decent job so that I could take my mother and leave. I have a sister too, but my mother doesn't want to leave the family home. She is worried about . . .'

'I think I can understand your mother's concerns. Many in our society still judge women who are separated from their husbands and she's probably concerned about how that might impact her daughters' marriage prospects.'

'You are right, ma'am. She says that I should go abroad and never come back to India. She wants me to get married to a good man irrespective of his caste and creed. Her only condition is that he mustn't drink. But I don't want to run away and leave my mother and sister behind. I want to be here for them. I'm so confused, ma'am. That's the reason why I wanted your advice.'

The word AA was on my mind. 'What is AA?' I asked.

'Alcoholics Anonymous. It is a support group for men and women who are addicted to alcohol. It has taken my father several years to become sober, but the darkness he caused has left a permanent scar on my heart and life. I don't like to share anything personal with him nor do I ask him for advice. I have no respect for him at all.'

'Jaya, I don't know much about AA, but we don't know the circumstances under which he turned to the bottle. He has changed now and it sounds like he is trying hard to be a better man. The best way forward is not to get upset or run away from your problems, but to open a channel of conversation with him. Your father must regret the actions of his past. Is he nice to your mother now?'

'Of course, he has been very good to her since he became sober.'

I sensed that she was feeling better. 'Jaya, go to a counsellor with him and work things out. Having a third party helps in seeing things clearer. You can defer your admission for a year and start working here. After that time has passed, re-evaluate your life by yourself or with the help of a counsellor and you will make the right decision. In a lifespan of many years, you can take time off for a year to figure out what's good for you. It is worth it.'

She smiled and her eyes shone brightly. She thanked me and left.

That day, my thoughts were preoccupied with AA. At the foundation, we are already predisposed to reaching out to people in tough situations. Dharma, on its own, also means protecting someone who needs it, no matter who they are or where they come from. It's pure and simple, and my mind wouldn't rest easy. Besides, we had never worked on this problem before and I had to understand it first. I got some information on AA online but it wasn't sufficient. Multiple questions bounced around in my mind. What was it and how did it really play a role in an alcoholic's life? What challenges does he or she face? Was it hereditary? Does one's financial status or family make a difference? How does counselling help? What is the success rate of de-addiction and where does a person go on from there?

It was clear—I needed first-hand information. I wanted to meet someone to understand the problem a little better. Vaguely, I recalled a friend mentioning in passing many years ago that her son-in-law had been a victim of this. I hadn't been good at keeping in touch and wondered if he would speak to me about it.

I took a chance, picked up the phone and reached out to my friend. I was hesitant. When she came on the line, we chatted for a few minutes and tried to catch up on the time gone by. Finally, I asked her, 'Several years ago, you had told me about your son-in-law, Ramesh, and that he had gone to a de-addiction camp. How is he doing now?'

'With God's grace and with the help of AA, he is sober now and lives a good life.'

'Would he mind if I asked him a few questions about the group? Only if he wants to, of course. I can assure you that it will remain confidential.'

'Sure, I will talk to him about it. I will message you his number if he agrees,' said my friend.

'Thank you!'

Within ten minutes, I received his contact details and immediately called him. The man on the other side of the phone sounded like he was around forty years old.

'Aunty!' said Ramesh, his voice full of warmth. 'I am happy to know that you want to hear about AA. I will share my journey with you and you can write about it too, if you like. It'll be worth it even if one person learns from my mistakes.'

'Why don't you come over for a meal? We can speak leisurely then,' I suggested.

Soon, we decided to meet in my house for lunch.

He was on time and confident in his demeanour. We sat down at the table. There was no need for polite conversation or formalities.

'Tell me about your experience with AA,' I broached the subject without beating around the bush.

'I've read your book titled *The Day I Stopped Drinking Milk*. But if I had to write one, it would be called *The Day I Began Drinking Alcohol*.' He sighed. 'Let me tell you how it all began.

'I belong to a conservative family. As children, we were expected to be home by sunset and were not allowed even tea or coffee! The only liquids I was allowed were milk, water and *teertha* (holy water). I was an excellent student and finished my twelfth grade with outstanding marks.

'A few days later, some of my classmates and I decided to celebrate. We went to a restaurant and ordered a round of drinks. I had never tried alcohol before and it was a close friend, a coffee planter's son from Coorg, who egged me on. "Come on, have a drink! Social drinking is quite acceptable now and it does absolutely no harm. One or two drinks will make you happier than the high you must have got from your top marks! Take this," he said and handed me a peg of whisky with ice cubes.

'Most of us were first-timers. Though the taste of the drink was slightly bitter, we all drank and felt good and relaxed. For some time, I felt that I was floating on air. The music was good and the world around me seemed beautiful and I had a nice buzz. I liked it.

'The evening turned into night and we ordered dinner. Though I was a foodie then, I didn't feel like eating anything. Instead, I quietly went to the bar and took a second peg. Everyone at the table clapped, "You were so cautious first, but look at you now!"

'The night ended on a high note and my friend dropped me home in his car. Since it was late, my parents were already asleep, so I used my key to enter the house and crashed on the bed.

'The next morning, I didn't stir until 7.30 a.m. When I opened my eyes, the sun's rays were shining brightly through the window.

'It was late. I usually woke up at 6 a.m.

'When my mother saw me, she asked, "Are you unwell?"

'I shook my head, but my head was feeling heavy and I had a slight headache.

'"How was the party?"

'"It was fine."

'I headed to the bathroom for a shower and felt slightly better. I went about my routine and at the end of the day, I thought about alcohol. I was fascinated by the high it had brought me.

'A few days later, I wanted to drink again and called my friend. He laughed and said, "No problem, man. Let's have another party."

'This time, it was only the two of us. My friend taught me about the different kinds of alcohol, the qualities and the prices, as I eagerly awaited my peg. We began meeting regularly and without realizing it, I got addicted to alcohol and began yearning for it every day.

'A month later, I got admission in a college in Mumbai and left home. Now I had complete freedom and there was absolutely no one to control me. I began boozing with different classmates. Somehow, I still managed to get decent grades, despite bunking classes—either due to hangovers or because I had slept late the previous night. I even got a good job that paid me well. Unfortunately for me, it also meant that I began drinking more since I could afford more.

'A few years later, I was transferred to Bengaluru. By then, my parents had built another house on the floor upstairs and I told them that I'd like to stay there. I had an arranged marriage and the girl was very nice. But once my wife began living with me, she learnt of my addiction within a few days. Livid, she fought with my poor parents, thinking that they were aware of my alcoholism and had chosen to hide it from her.

'My mother was horrified! She had had no knowledge of my addiction. The only symptom she was aware of was that I had become short-tempered, but she had innocently attributed it to the stress at my workplace. I had, of course, let her think that way. So along with my wife, I got a sermon every day and it greatly annoyed me. She dragged me to temples and gurus. The more they pushed me, the more upset I became. Through it all, my wife continued to believe in me. "You are intelligent," she would say. "You can leave this habit. I know you can control your urges."

'Sometimes her words gave me strength, but I couldn't let go of alcohol.'

I was dumbfounded. This could happen to anyone, especially in this day and age. I stopped him. 'Tell me, how did you find out about AA?'

'Now you must understand my journey, Aunty. Day after day, it became worse and I kept drowning in the problem that I had created. One day, I got a call from my old friend from Coorg. He was visiting Bengaluru with his cousin and invited me to his hotel. I was happy to hear from him and thought that we could have a memorable evening together. When I eventually saw him, I was concerned. The young, handsome boy looked like an old man and a skeleton at that!

'"Shall we order something to drink?" I asked, a few minutes into our meeting.

'"Don't even mention the word alcohol. It is killing me. For a long time, I refused to get married. My parents tried their best to rescue me from this life, but now I have been diagnosed with liver cirrhosis. I can't tell you how much I regret the past! I was born into a good family and grew up in a wonderful place like Coorg where I could have done something meaningful. People always plan a holiday there and I already lived in heaven. I should have become high on nature, but instead I became high on alcohol. I don't have much time left. Don't waste your life, old friend! Learn from me. A man near his death will always tell you the bare truth. This disease is worse than cancer. People will sympathize with you if you have cancer and there are medicines and surgeries that might give you a chance to get back to your old life. But here I am. This is what rock bottom looks like. People look down on me and judge me, even my parents. I thank God that I am not married or I would have ruined another person's life too."

'His words threw me for a loop. How could this have happened to him? This isn't how life is supposed to turn out for people like us.

'I came home and tossed and turned all night. I couldn't stop thinking about him or myself. My life was a mess.

Sometimes, I would skip work because I had drunk too much the previous day. People who were less smart than me were getting promoted and I was being passed over again and again because I wasn't considered reliable enough. Meanwhile, my wife and mother were under our relatives' constant scrutiny because of my condition. It was plain as day—I wasn't that far off from being in the same boat as my friend. The very idea shook me to the core.

'The next morning, there was a call from my friend's hotel. It was his cousin. "Your friend passed away last night," he said. "You were his last visitor."

'I began trembling with shock and fear. It was the lowest point of my life, and I couldn't control my body from shivering. When the shivers stopped, I went to the small cupboard containing all the alcohol, took the bottles and threw them in the trash.

'With the help of my family, I learnt about AA and checked in to the alcohol de-addiction camp. It took a few years for me to become sober and I have been this way ever since. I now dedicate my life to helping others who are in a bad place because of alcoholism. I work with them and show them that there is hope. They can get better.'

He stopped and opened the bag he was carrying. He rummaged in it for a few seconds and took a book out. He handed it to me. 'This is a book on AA and their twelve steps. They include apologizing to those we have hurt, helping others and surrendering to God.'

I took the book from him, eager to read it.

'Aunty, I am ashamed of my past but I am also proud that I could leave it behind me. My wife and mother have played an important role in bringing me back.'

I was amazed to learn so much! He had opened a new door for me.

'Please attend one AA meeting, Aunty!' he said. 'There are two types of meetings—open and closed. Anyone can go for the open ones while the closed gatherings are only for the members. Tomorrow, there is an open session in Electronic City where I am the chairman.'

'Chairman?' I asked out aloud.

'Yes, but not in the regular sense of the word. A chairman here is a mentor who shares his experience, the challenges of his journey and the weak moments too. He also gives input to the members on how to conquer the desire of a few minutes so that the person can survive the urge to drink.'

I said, 'I would like to join you tomorrow. You have shared your story because you know me, but why will other people want to share their darkest moments with me?'

'Once I have the other members' permission to let you in for an open session, then it will not be a problem. Most of them are willing to speak about it because now they recognize the problem and genuinely want to become sober. They don't know how to go about it and that's where AA comes in,' he explained patiently.

'Now that you are a mentor yourself, what about you? Whom do you speak to?'

He smiled and said, 'I continue to have a mentor and visit him weekly. I am human, after all.'

The conversation took a different turn and we spoke about philosophy for some time. When the time came for him to leave, he said, 'See you tomorrow. I will text you the location of the church.'

'Why are you meeting there?' I was curious.

'Aunty, where else can we meet? In a place like Bengaluru, thirty of us cannot fit into an average-sized living room. If we look for places on hire, then the payments have to be budgeted. When we ask people to make an exception or allow us to use their facilities for minimal or no cost, they immediately refuse when they learn of the purpose. We were running out of places to meet and so we approached a church. The management was kind enough to allow us to use a space in their premises.'

I thanked the church authorities in my head for comprehending human nature and allowing sins to be forgiven. It is the essence of life.

'They said we could donate whatever we could afford but insisted that we keep the place clean.'

'Why did they say that? Do people get their drinks there?' I asked innocently.

'Aunty, come on. AA is about not drinking and that's what the whole session is about. A lot of people who drink also smoke. If we consider drug addiction to be one of three brothers, then it is the worst of them all. Alcohol comes next, while smoking is the youngest of the three. The elder brother is usually accompanied by the two younger ones, while the middle brother almost always appears with the youngest. So we keep ashtrays on a table and clean up before we leave.'

'Who funds these meetings? Can Infosys Foundation help?'

'Thanks, Aunty, but AA doesn't take help from anyone on that front,' he replied.

Soon, Ramesh left.

The next day, I reached the venue, a Christian school, at the assigned time. There was a small crowd of both men and women standing outside. The evening was fading away and night was almost upon us.

Suddenly, I felt awkward. At times, being a writer has its negatives. What if someone questioned my presence?

'Why did she come?'

'Is she going to write about us?'

Just then, Ramesh called me inside. He said that he wouldn't be taking the session that day. I entered the room and sat in a corner. It was a regular classroom with tables and benches—there were no DVDs, overhead projector or any fancy equipment.

Within five minutes, the room was full. There were people of different ages and genders, though the number of girls and women was less than the number of men. There were some foreigners too. A group of students entered and announced their presence before retreating to another corner of the room. No one paid any attention to me, but I still felt out of my depth.

A middle-aged person walked in firmly and greeted everyone. Then he sat down in the front, facing us. He opened a book and read out the twelve steps that I had learnt about the day before. I observed some faces looking tense and worried. After that was done, the chairman said, 'Welcome to all fellow members, guests and students. This is an open session. Today, I'd like to share something good. Fellow Bharat, where are you?'

A man in his forties raised his hand.

'Bharat is completing his first birthday here. We will cut the cake at the end of the session.'

Everyone clapped. I didn't understand what was going on. What did the chairman mean by saying it was his first birthday?

'Our guests today may be a little surprised to see this celebration, but the first birthday is a very big deal. It means that Bharat hasn't had alcohol for a year now.'

'So that's what it is,' I thought.

'As the chairman, I will share my experience first. My initiation and drinking began in college under peer pressure. It was cool to drink and I was proud to be in the party crowd. Over the next few years, I became an alcoholic. Still, I was able to land a job, find a good girl and gain appreciation for my work. When I thought the time was right, I asked my girlfriend to marry me, but she refused. She said that I was drunk whenever she met me, irrespective of the time of the day. So I turned to the bottle even more, using my heartbreak as an excuse.

'One day, my parents finally said to me, "Grow up! The girl left you years ago and is now the mother of two children and yet, here you are—still drinking your life away. This has nothing to do with her and everything to do with you—you are an alcoholic. We are ready to help you get your life back on track, but you must realize what you have become."

'I was livid. How dare they label me an alcoholic? I could quit drinking whenever I wanted to. I was the one in control. So I didn't drink for the next two days and thought that I had proved myself. On the third day, my parents wanted to go to a temple nearby and I offered to drive them there. I had a quick shower in the evening, shaved and applied an aftershave lotion. I looked good.

'A short time later, we left for the temple. While driving, my tongue touched my skin briefly and it tasted of the aftershave lotion. I kept licking it and by the time we reached the temple, I was craving for a drink. I dropped my parents, went to the closest bar and stayed there for four hours. Unaware of my actions, my poor parents performed a puja for me at the temple, waited for me, then took an autorickshaw and went back home.

'That was my turning point. It was the day I realized that I couldn't live without booze. So I came to AA and they helped me vocalize what I was. It was here that I found other people like me and I was glad that I wasn't alone in this. Our slogan is "I can't, we can".'

The chairman looked straight at the crowd in front of him, 'If you would like to stay and be with us, please do so. You are always welcome here. People who think that this isn't the place for them, let me tell you that there is a bar on the opposite side of the street. Feel free to leave.'

He paused, waiting for people to exit. One person did, but at a turtle's pace.

Then he said, 'Only an alcoholic can understand another fellow alcoholic. Nobody is going to judge you here. I invite you to share your experience or thoughts.'

By then, the environment felt very informal and I didn't feel awkward any more.

A young lady sitting on one of the benches introduced herself. 'I am Raveena Alcoholic,' she said.

'Hi, Raveena Alcoholic,' responded the other members.

'I come from an affluent family where social drinking was a part of our culture. My parents studied in France and hence frequently discussed wine and its various characteristics. I was introduced to wine at the age of sixteen but the quantity was restricted. The next year, I went to college in Delhi and my parents headed to the Middle East for a financially exciting job opportunity. I stayed back in a residential hostel where I met girls who frequently drank hard liquor such as vodka and whisky. At first, they made fun of me and urged me to try what they were having. So I began experimenting and came to love other drinks too. My parents used to send me a monthly allowance then. Whenever they asked me about my spending, I would conceal my expenses on alcohol. Lying came naturally to me once I started it and I barely felt guilty about it over time.'

'There comes the fourth brother,' I thought.

'Around the time of my graduation, I went to a bar and met a boy. We got along like a house on fire and spent a lot of time learning about each other and our habits. We disclosed our relationship to our parents who approved of the match and we had a lavish wedding. Following the north Indian tradition, there was plenty of wine and liquor on the day of the reception, and the guests drank as much as possible since it was free. After the wedding, my husband and I shifted to Bengaluru. We would sit and drink together every day after he returned from work, but he noticed that I could drink more than him. I needed more than two pegs to get high and I didn't puke afterwards or get a headache immediately either. I thought it was a great quality and that I must push myself further.'

Suddenly, Raveena's voice softened. 'Weeks later, I learnt that I was pregnant and went to a gynaecologist. I didn't tell her about the alcohol. During the third month of pregnancy, I felt very uneasy in the area around my stomach and went to see her again.

'As a part of the routine check-up, she asked me, "Are you drinking alcohol? Perhaps wine?"

'"Wine," I said, concealing the hard liquor I was still downing every now and then.

'"Stop it."

'I tried to but I couldn't control myself. "Doctors are extra careful about these things," I thought. "A sip here and there isn't going to harm the baby."

'So I poured myself some vodka and orange juice the very next day, and continued to drink with my husband.

'Nine months later, a baby boy was born and our families were ecstatic. Everybody celebrated with wine and champagne in our house but it wasn't enough for me.

I needed more. Taking care of a newborn was much more exhausting than I had thought. When the parents had retired for the night to their bedrooms, I went to the mini-bar in the dining room and drank vodka.

'A year passed and my son grew up quickly. I noticed that his milestones were delayed and ran to the doctor. Within a month, it was confirmed—my son was a slow learner and would remain so. The doctor remarked, "I hope you weren't drinking during the pregnancy."

'That hit home. The drinking hadn't harmed me but it had labelled my child "special". He had done nothing to deserve this and yet, he was the one paying for my sins.

'I could not excuse myself and felt like ending my life, but the thought of my son prevented me from taking a step further. If I wasn't around, who would look after him? What does his future hold? My husband and I didn't blame each other, but ourselves. We took strength from each other and decided to quit drinking. It was very hard and we kept failing at our attempts. We ended up drinking in the evenings, just like we used to before.

'Thankfully, we found AA and now that's the time I keep for my meetings. The withdrawal was painful and difficult. Once the evening is past, I am more in control and I return home. My son's face is a stark reminder of why I must never touch a drink again. Why did God make such an addictive thing on earth?' Her voice shook with the emotions that she kept bottled inside her. 'I am scared to have another baby. What if I get another child like my son?'

The chairman stepped in, 'Thank you, Raveena Alcoholic, for sharing your personal story. People come to AA when they reach the lowest point in their lives. That point differs from person to person. We had one teenager who once asked his mother for money to buy alcohol. When she refused to part with it, he pushed her and damaged her leg. In time, she developed a limp. It was an eternal reminder to the son about how he had hurt her and it became his turning point. Once people desperately desire a change in the most honest way possible, they come here because we can help them make it happen.'

Next, a well-dressed middle-aged man in the front row introduced himself. He said, 'I am Harry Alcoholic and belong to a wealthy family. I have no excuse. I got the habit because I enjoyed drinking with my friends. Since my father had his own business, I decided to join him after my graduation and fell in love with one of the secretaries named Maria. She learnt of my weaknesses and about the drinking too. As time passed, we seriously began thinking of marriage.

'"I want you to quit drinking," she told me. "With God's grace and love, you will leave it, I'm sure."

'At first, my parents were hesitant about the match but soon they took to Maria and we had a big fat wedding. Still, I continued to drink. Two years later, my mother and father died in a car crash and I was the only one to inherit all that they had built. I managed the office and Maria managed everything at home, including the finances. We also had a beautiful baby girl and life was wonderful. Yet, my habit continued.

'When Maria spoke to me about it, I didn't heed her words. Every day, I would ask her for money to spend at the bar. One day, she put her foot down, "No, you won't get any more money for this. I decided to marry you in the hope that you would improve and because I loved you. You are the same, despite becoming a father."

'I became so upset that I abused her verbally and told her that the money was mine and that she had no right over it. With tears in her eyes, she handed me some money and I rushed to the bar. The next morning, I felt bad and apologized to her, "I'm so sorry, Maria, I was wrong. I will never do it again."

'But I did. Again and again.

'One day, the same incident repeated itself and Maria refused to give me money. I saw my daughter playing on the side and yelled at Maria with hate, "If you don't give me what I want, I will do something to the baby and then you will regret it."

'I was in complete rage. That's the only reason I said it. I loved my daughter more than my life.

'But Maria turned pale. She probably thought I meant it. She brought out all the money she had and handed it to me. "Take it," she said and walked out of the room with my daughter.

'I took all the money, called a few friends and went to a popular bar that I frequented and whose owner I knew. People would often join me there and praise my gracious nature because I paid for everyone's drinks. But in my heart, I was still mad at Maria. I wanted to show her that I was not a henpecked husband, so I drank more than usual that day. The owner allowed me to crash in a room above the bar because I wasn't in any state to walk or drive.

'When I came home the next morning, there was a note on the fridge. It was a handwritten note from Maria.

I am leaving with my daughter. You will never change. You may have ruined my life, but I don't want my daughter's to be ruined too with a drunk man for a father.

'I looked around the apartment. All their clothes were gone.

'But I knew she would come back. To forget my domestic problems, I began drinking even more. Maria, however, didn't turn up at all. Weeks turned into months and months into years. I didn't know where she was any more.

'Within a few years, I lost everything—my business and my properties.

'Now, the owner of that same popular bar instructed the bouncers not to let me in without money. My friends forgot about me too. It got worse and I began begging at traffic lights. All the money I got went into buying and consuming desi liquor.

'One day, I sat at a traffic signal and thought that I saw Maria in one of the cabs with a child. When I went closer, I realized that it really was her, along with my daughter. Excited, I knocked at the car window. She, however, dismissed me with a wave of her hand. "Never talk to strangers," she said to our daughter. "Look at this dirty man begging here instead of working somewhere."

'She didn't recognize me! Before I could find any words, the light turned green and the car sped away.

'That was the lowest point in my life—I had lost my wife, daughter and what my parents and grandparents had built for me. My family had had a humble beginning. My grandfather had come from Kolar to Bengaluru city as a clerk, worked very hard and saved money to start his own business. It took decades for him to officially reach the "rich" status. His name was Harry and I had been named after him. But look at me! I had squandered away all his wealth and become a beggar. I wanted to commit suicide right there and then.

'I don't remember how but someone took me to an open AA session in a church and for the first time in many years, I felt a ray of hope. I heard people talking about their darkest times. They were people like me who had lost everything and then gone on to build a decent life for themselves. Maybe I could try too. It's been fifteen years since then and I have been sober for a long time. Now I spend my life in service to others like me by bringing them to AA and helping them on their journey.'

The applause in the room was followed by a deafening silence, each of us busy with our own thoughts.

'His daughter must be working now and maybe married too!' I thought. 'His wife is a brave woman. She made the right decision for herself and the child, but what a life they have all led. Everyone has suffered a lifetime because of alcohol addiction.'

I didn't know if alcoholism was a formally recognized medical disease, but AA was a boon for the people it served.

Coffee was served in paper cups for all of us, and a stringed purse and a round medal was circulated. The chairman announced, 'You can contribute only if you are AA members. We don't accept money from others.'

A few contributed and most of the members took the medal, held it close to their heart and prayed.

At last, the chairman invited Bharat to come and cut the cake. 'We have also invited Bharat's family today because he wouldn't have reached this milestone without them,' he said.

With pride, Bharat blew out the lone candle on it and cut the cake. Then he thanked his family profusely along with the people in AA who had given him back his life.

His father then handed him a medal. He was speechless, choked with emotion. After he had composed himself, he said, 'Bharat is my only child and I have celebrated many events with him, including his birthdays and wedding. But today is his real birthday. For a long time, I was ashamed to have a son like him but he has changed and I am a proud father.'

Bharat smiled and patted his father's shoulder and looked at the small gathering with gratitude. 'An alcoholic is an alcoholic forever,' he said. 'I cannot take any medicines with alcoholic content, not even a spoonful of cough syrup when I am unwell. But I am happy with where I am right now and I promise I will continue to celebrate such birthdays every year.'

I glanced at Bharat's wife who stood nearby. It had been no cakewalk for her with the kind of pressure society often forces on Indian women. She had had a troublesome marriage without true companionship and was still standing beside her husband.

A few minutes later, the meeting got over and people started leaving. I also stood up and Ramesh accompanied me to the car waiting outside.

'Does everyone reach sobriety?' I asked Ramesh.

'It depends, Aunty. There are chances of relapsing. That's why we meet regularly to keep our urges in control. Even now, when I see an alcohol ad or a drinking scene in a movie on television, I switch it off. I don't go to any wedding that serves liquor. It is very easy to fall off the wagon. Surrendering to God, which is one of the steps in AA, is very helpful. God doesn't mean a specific religious one. Everyone has a God within themselves. It simply means a higher power. In AA, we have the freedom of choosing our God. It is a great organization and Bengaluru alone has eighty centres. AA operates in 186 countries. Aunty, no wonder our ancestors were intelligent. They told us to keep away from bad habits. It may start as social drinking but unfortunately, some get hooked to it. And once they are hooked, their life becomes miserable. If they had not tried it in the first place, they would not have become alcoholics.'

I sat in the car and thought about the famous Marathi play *Ekach Pyala*, a popular drama of the 1940s, and another one called *Devadas*, which is a play about a man who, as people like to believe, turned to the bottle because he could not marry Paro, the love of his life. But the truth is that he was simply an alcoholic.

In the Marathi play, the protagonist, Sudhakar, and his wife, Sindhu, are a happy couple. One day, an alcoholic friend insists that Sudhakar should drink one sip of alcohol to celebrate an event. He even offers him a peg. Sindhu objects to her husband's drinking, who mocks her, 'O Sindhu, don't worry. Our life's ship will not drown with one peg.'

Unfortunately, her husband likes the taste and in time, becomes a slave to alcohol. The play shows how their life is ruined. The first peg is enough to get you on the journey, if you have a tendency towards alcoholism. Unfortunately, nobody can predict until you try that first glass.

Who says money is the ultimate goal of life? It isn't. You will find out when the time is right.

One of life's goals is the ability to understand human nature and raise a fellow being from rock bottom to becoming a useful member of society. We all lose a few battles in our lives, but we can win the war.

There's always hope.